William J.
Standiford

INDIVIDUAL LIBERTY & SOCIETAL FREEDOM

THE MAKING OF A
A FREE SOCIETY

Author's Note:

The principles of the constitution outline the principles of Freedom, and should be regarded as such. In assessing the current political climate & cultural divisions, there is no doubt that understanding the constitution as it is written (as well as its implied context) is becoming ever-so important for citizens of our country.

The constitution of the United States was written as a framework - a guiding tool to highlight exactly how our government should function, what our government can and cannot do, and the constraints associated with drafting new legislation. To know your rights is the ability to protect & preserve your freedom. Rights are like muscles…if you don't exercise them, they'll lose their strength.

These are the foundational ideas that led to the creation of this book, 'Individual Liberty &

Societal Freedom.' This book is not just another exploration of constitutional theory; it is a passionate call to action and an open invitation to engage in a crucial conversation about the very essence of our nation's existence.

In the pages that follow, we will embark on a journey through the intricate web of constitutional principles, exploring how they serve as the bedrock of individual liberty and societal freedom. This book seeks to shed light on the critical importance of protecting the original framework of the constitution, a document that has guided our nation through centuries of growth, change, and challenge.

Throughout this book, we will delve into the stories, examples, and historical context that highlight the real-world implications of constitutional integrity on our lives. We will discuss the struggles and triumphs of those who have fought to protect and preserve our constitutional rights. And most importantly, we will examine how each one of us, as citizens, can play an active role in upholding the principles of freedom and justice.

So, dear reader, expect to be enlightened, challenged, and empowered. Expect to gain a deeper understanding of the constitution's role in safeguarding our individual liberty and societal freedom. Expect to discover the tools you need to exercise your rights effectively, ensuring they remain as strong as ever.

As you embark on this journey through 'Individual Liberty & Societal Freedom,' remember that the constitution is not merely a historical document; it is a living, breathing testament to the values upon which our nation was founded. Its principles resonate today as they did when ink first met parchment. It is our duty to protect and uphold these principles, and through this book, you will find the knowledge and inspiration to do just that.

PREFACE

Constitutional Integrity is a subject that is quite misunderstood. The principles of the constitution outline the principles of Freedom, and should be regarded as such. In assessing the current political climate & cultural divisions, there is no doubt that understanding the constitution as it is written (as well as its implied context) is becoming ever-so important for citizens of our country. The constitution of the United States was written as a framework - a guiding tool to highlight exactly how our government should function, what our government can and cannot do, and the constraints associated with drafting new legislation. To know your rights is the ability to protect & preserve your freedom. Rights are like muscles…if you don't exercise them, they'll lose their strength.

Part of my writing this novel is to have an open discussion about the importance of protecting the original framework of the constitution. Our modern climate has provided the perfect circumstances for the violation of our civil rights. Primarily due to ignorance of these rights, we (as citizens) have allowed our policing forces to enforce the feelings of others - opposed to upholding the jurisdictional statutes, and ultimately upholding the integrity of the U.S. Constitution. Did you realize that there can be no law that exists which conflicts with the U.S. Constitution? It's true! Any law which conflicts with the constitution for all intents & purposes is considered null & void…it will not be upheld by the judicial system, should a law conflict with what the constitution states on the matter.

It is reprehensible that "Peace Officers" would disregard the framework that is the constitution, as law enforcement officers have a great responsibility to check the integrity of a law against the constitution, as laws conflicting with the constitution (which peace officers take an oath to uphold) should not be enforced. Officers of the law have a great responsibility to continuously educate themselves and their colleagues, to accurately enforce the law. More than that, they should be willing to admit their ignorance of the law, but be willing to do the appropriate research to find out the reality of the law - so that it may be enforced peacefully and fairly.

Officers of the law are meant to uphold the law, meaning peace officers are under the scope of the law, not above the law. To "uphold" something is to confirm or provide support…officers cannot support the integrity of the law if they are actively breaking it themselves.

The founders were often referred to as the "framers" of the constitution. After years of failed governance by the Articles of Confederation due to a lack of central governance (Federal Power), the constitution was put together as a basic framework by which a strong central government could operate within. This framework was established as a means to protect the governed from the government; through consent of the governed, checked with the legal allowances provided by the constitution, operates a strong central government which operates to every citizen's benefit. When the checks and balances of the constitutional framework given to us is abused, tyranny is in operation. Tyranny, by simple definition, is cruel, unreasonable, or arbitrary use of power or control.

Many of the problems within government today are due to a lack of checks and balances. In essence, the system of checks and balances our constitution highlights have been consistently undermined by the abuse of authority by lawmakers. Lawmakers have been churning out left & right laws which conflict with the framework of the constitution. Theoretically, the supreme court's job is to "filter" these laws against the constitution, and any laws which conflict with the ideology of the constitution are to be considered null & void. However, with the Supreme Court realistically only able to hear a certain number of cases per year, it's becoming exceedingly difficult to filter the hundreds of laws that are passed each year. As a result, many laws which should be considered null & void when checked against the framework of the constitution go unchecked and are considered legal, when in fact they should be tossed out/discarded - in the name of preserving personal liberty and civil rights.

With regard to current affairs, at the time of writing this publication, the Supreme Court is facing a highly politicized decision to uphold or strike down the Biden Student Loan Forgiveness plan. The high court's decision on this matter will ultimately affect the finances of millions of Americans, and includes a high price tag to

American taxpayers…bringing into question the constitutionality of the Biden Administration's policy regarding student loan forgiveness.

If the 2003 congress did in fact intend on allowing the Department of Education to permanently discharge student loan balances with the passing of the HEROS Act (Higher Education Relief Opportunities for Students Act of 2003), it would be because of the language used in the passing of this law was to allow the Department of Education to 'Waive & Modify' policies regarding student loan balances.

Under ideal circumstances where every branch of government is acting with upright moral capacity, this case would likely be pretty cut and dry. If the language used in the HEROS Act of 2003 allows for the waiving and modification of student loan balances, that *should* include forgiveness, as that would be a *permanent waiver/modification* of student balances. Due to the deep political division in the United States, however; this case has become another "hot" debate, like Roe v. Wade - and drives another wedge between conservatives and liberals…only deeping the political divide of the country.

If the court were to review the case with regard to the objective facts of the matter, then in fact, there would be no reason to strike down the plan - as congress clearly provided authority to the Department of Education in 2003 to modify these balances in the event of economic emergencies. I would say the COVID-19 pandemic certainly was a significant enough public health, as well as primarily an economic emergency. Never in our modern age have governments spent over 5 trillion dollars of taxpayer money in less than 2 years…there was an unprecedented amount of relief provided to millions of Americans during the pandemic, which ultimately brought us to our current economic situation of rampant inflation.

The United States Supreme Court is responsible to the American people for determining the authority of Congress, as well as the Executive branch. Their job is to decipher the constitution, and strike down laws that conflict with it..as the constitution is the ' 'Supreme law of the land" in the United States; meaning, no law, in any jurisdiction, can exist while in conflict with the constitution. Any law which does exist which is in conflict with the parameters of the constitution should be considered void, and should be contested through the judiciary to publicly determine its constitutionality.

In short, congress cannot ethically pass laws conflicting with the constitution. Sure, in theory they can pass any law, but the Supreme Court will ultimately make a final decision on its constitutionality, and will void any law that is unconstitutional.

With regard to our current socio-economic & political environment, freedom has become such a strained ideal, that I'm not entirely certain the average person could tell you we're still living in a free society.

INTRODUCTION

The United States Constitution is the supreme law of the land in the United States of America. It was created to establish a stronger, more effective federal government and provide a framework for governing the country. The Constitution is the foundation of the American government and the source of all legal authority. Its historical significance is immeasurable, as it has played a key role in shaping American democracy and has served as a model for democratic governments around the world.

The United States Constitution was drafted and adopted in 1787. This was a time when the United States was still a young and fragile nation, and the Articles of Confederation, which had been the country's first constitution, had proven to be ineffective in governing the country. Under the Articles, the federal government had limited powers, and the individual states had too much autonomy, which created problems in areas such as commerce, taxation, and national defense. A group of delegates, known as the Founding Fathers, met in Philadelphia in the summer of 1787 to address these problems and to draft a new constitution that would create a stronger federal government and provide a framework for governing the country.

The drafting of the Constitution was a complex and contentious process that took several months to complete. The delegates at the Constitutional Convention had to work out a number of difficult issues, such as how to balance the power of the federal government with the rights of the states, how to structure the federal government, and how to ensure that the rights of individual citizens were protected. After several months of debate and compromise, the delegates finally agreed on a new Constitution.

The next step was to get the Constitution ratified by the individual states. This proved to be a difficult task, as many people were skeptical of the new Constitution and feared that it would create a centralized government that would be too powerful. The supporters of the Constitution, known as Federalists, argued that the new Constitution was necessary to ensure the stability and prosperity of the country. They launched a campaign to persuade the states to ratify the Constitution, which involved writing a series of essays known as the Federalist Papers. In the end, the Constitution was ratified by all 13 states and became the supreme law of the land on March 4, 1789.

The Constitution establishes a federal system of government, which means that power is divided between the federal government and the individual states. The federal government is composed of three branches: the legislative branch, which is responsible for making laws; the executive branch, which is responsible for enforcing laws; and the judicial branch, which is responsible for interpreting laws. Each branch has its own specific powers and responsibilities and is designed to provide a system of checks and balances to prevent any one branch from becoming too powerful.

The legislative branch, or Congress, is made up of the House of Representatives and the Senate. The House of Representatives has 435 members who are elected every two years. The number of representatives from each state is based on the state's population. The Senate has 100 members, two from each state, who are elected for six-year terms. The main responsibility of Congress is to make laws, and it has the power to levy taxes, regulate commerce, and declare war.

The executive branch is headed by the President, who is elected for a four-year term. The President is responsible for enforcing the laws passed by

Congress and has the power to veto laws that he or she disagrees with. The President also has the power to appoint federal judges and other government officials, subject to the approval of the Senate.

The judicial branch is made up of the Supreme Court and other federal courts. The Supreme Court is the highest court in the land and has the power to interpret the Constitution and to review the constitution. The U.S. Constitution plays a crucial role in protecting freedom in America through its separation of powers, individual rights protections, and flexibility for future generations.

The Constitution is extremely relevant to modern tyranny and individual freedom, as it provides a framework for protecting the rights and freedoms of individuals and preventing tyranny and abuse of power by the government.

One of the most important ways that the Constitution protects individual freedom is through the Bill of Rights, the first ten amendments to the Constitution. The Bill of Rights guarantees certain basic rights and freedoms, such as freedom of speech, religion, and the press, as well as the right to bear arms, the right to a fair trial, and protection against unreasonable searches and seizures. These rights are essential to individual freedom and have been upheld by the Supreme Court in numerous cases over the years.

The Constitution also provides a system of checks and balances that is designed to prevent any one branch of government from becoming too powerful and abusing its authority. For example, the President has the power to veto laws passed by Congress, but Congress can override the veto with a two-thirds vote. Similarly, the Supreme Court has the power to strike down laws that it deems unconstitutional, but Congress can override the Court by amending the Constitution.

Another way that the Constitution protects individual freedom is by establishing federalism, the system of government in which power is divided between the federal government and the states. This allows states to have a certain degree of autonomy and to make their own laws, which can help to protect individual freedom by providing a check against the power of the federal government.

The Constitution is also relevant to modern tyranny because it provides a mechanism for removing government officials who abuse their power or violate the Constitution. For example, the Constitution provides for impeachment of the President, Vice President, and other federal officials for "high crimes and misdemeanors." This mechanism has been used several times throughout history to remove officials who have abused their power or violated the Constitution.

In recent years, there has been concern about the potential for government overreach and abuse of power, particularly in the areas of surveillance and civil liberties. The Constitution provides a framework for addressing these concerns, including the Fourth Amendment's protections against unreasonable searches and seizures and the Fifth Amendment's protections against self-incrimination and double jeopardy.

CHAPTER 1: SEPARATION OF POWERS

The U.S. Constitution establishes a system of government with three branches: the legislative branch, the executive branch, and the judicial branch. Each branch has a specific set of responsibilities and powers that are designed to work together to provide a system of checks and balances that prevents any one branch from becoming too powerful.

The legislative branch, also known as Congress, is responsible for making laws. Congress is made up of two chambers: the House of Representatives and the Senate. The House of Representatives is based on proportional representation, with each state being represented based on its population. The Senate, on the other hand, has equal representation for each state, with two senators per state.

Congress has a number of important responsibilities. One of its most important powers is the power to make laws. This includes passing legislation, approving the federal budget, and approving treaties. Congress also has the power to impeach and remove the President, Vice President, and other federal officials from office for "high crimes and misdemeanors."

The legislative branch also plays a critical role in oversight of the other branches of government. Congress has the power to investigate the actions of the executive branch and to conduct oversight hearings to ensure that the executive branch is carrying out its responsibilities in accordance with the law. Additionally, Congress has the power of the purse, which means that it controls the funding for the executive branch and can use this power to influence executive branch policy decisions.

The executive branch is responsible for carrying out and enforcing the laws passed by Congress.

The President is the head of the executive branch, and is responsible for leading the country and managing its affairs. The President is also responsible for appointing federal judges, ambassadors, and other high-level officials.

The President has a number of important powers and responsibilities. One of the most important of these is the power to veto legislation passed by Congress. The President can also issue executive orders, which have the force of law and can be used to implement policy changes without going through Congress. Additionally, the President is responsible for leading the military and directing foreign policy.

The executive branch also includes a number of federal agencies, such as the Department of State, the Department of Defense, and the Department of Justice. These agencies are responsible for carrying out specific policy initiatives and enforcing federal laws. The executive branch also includes independent agencies, such as the Environmental Protection Agency, which are designed to be free from political interference.

The judicial branch is responsible for interpreting the laws and ensuring that they are applied fairly and consistently. The judicial branch is headed by the Supreme Court, which is the highest court in the land. The Supreme Court is made up of nine justices who are appointed by the President and approved by the Senate.

The judicial branch has a number of important responsibilities. One of the most important of these is interpreting the Constitution and determining whether laws are constitutional. This is known as judicial review, and is a critical aspect of the American legal system. The judicial branch also has the power to interpret federal laws and to resolve disputes between states.

The judicial branch also includes a number of lower courts, such as district courts and appellate courts. These courts are responsible for hearing cases and resolving disputes at the local level. The decisions made by these lower courts can be appealed to the Supreme Court if necessary.

One of the key features of the U.S. government is the system of checks and balances that is designed to prevent any one branch of government from becoming too powerful. Each branch has a specific set of powers and responsibilities that are designed to work together to create a balance of power.

Checks and balances are an essential part of the United States government, and they play a critical role in protecting individual freedoms and preventing abuses of power. The system of checks and balances is designed to ensure that no one branch of government becomes too powerful and that each branch has a specific set of powers and responsibilities that are designed to work together to create a balance of power.

One of the key benefits of the system of checks and balances is that it helps to prevent tyranny. The Founding Fathers were acutely aware of the dangers of centralized power, and they sought to create a system of government that would prevent any one person or group from gaining too much power. By distributing power among the legislative, executive, and judicial branches of government, the Constitution ensures that no one branch can dominate the others.

The system of checks and balances also helps to protect individual rights and freedoms. The Constitution guarantees a number of important rights, such as freedom of speech, religion, and the press, and the system of checks and balances ensures that these rights are protected. For example, the judiciary has the power to strike down laws that are unconstitutional, and the legislative branch can pass new laws to protect individual rights if they feel that existing laws are inadequate.

Another important benefit of checks and balances is that it helps to ensure accountability. By distributing power among multiple branches of government, the Constitution ensures that each branch is accountable to the others. This means that if one branch oversteps its bounds or abuses its power, the other branches can step in to rein it in. For example, the legislative branch has the power to impeach and remove the President from office if they believe that he has committed "high crimes and misdemeanors."

The system of checks and balances also promotes compromise and negotiation. Because no one branch of government can dominate the others, it is often necessary for the branches to work together to achieve their goals. This means that compromise and negotiation are essential components of the American political system. For example, the President may have to negotiate with Congress to pass important legislation, and the judiciary may have to work with the executive branch to implement court rulings.

The system of checks and balances is a fundamental aspect of the United States government that ensures that no one branch can become too powerful. This system divides the powers of government among the legislative, executive, and judicial branches, and each branch has a specific set of powers and responsibilities that are designed to work together to create a balance of power.

One of the most important checks and balances in the United States government is the power of the legislative branch to make laws. The Constitution grants the legislative branch, which is composed of the Senate and the House of Representatives, the power to create and pass laws. This power is a critical check on the executive branch, which is responsible for enforcing laws, and the judicial branch, which is responsible for interpreting laws.

The legislative branch can also check the power of the executive branch by overriding a presidential veto. If the President vetoes a bill, the legislative branch can vote to override the veto with a two-thirds majority vote in both the Senate and the House of Representatives. This power ensures that the President cannot simply veto any legislation he disagrees with, and it requires him to work with Congress to pass laws.

Similarly, the judicial branch has the power to check the power of the legislative and executive branches. The judicial branch, which is composed of the Supreme Court and other federal courts, has the power to interpret the Constitution and to strike down laws that are deemed unconstitutional. This power is an important check on the legislative branch, which may pass laws that violate individual rights or are outside the scope of their powers. The judicial branch can also check the power of the executive branch by ruling on the constitutionality of executive actions or orders.

The executive branch also has checks on its power. The Constitution grants the President the power to veto legislation, which is a significant check on the power of the legislative branch. However, the legislative branch can override the veto with a two-thirds majority vote in both the Senate and the House of Representatives. The executive branch is also subject to judicial review, which allows the courts to review the constitutionality of executive actions and orders.

The Watergate scandal was a political scandal that occurred in the 1970s during the presidency of Richard Nixon. The scandal involved the attempted cover-up of illegal activities, including the burglary of the Democratic National

Committee headquarters in the Watergate complex in Washington, D.C.

During the Watergate scandal, the separation of powers was put into action as the different branches of government worked to investigate the matter and hold those responsible accountable. The legislative branch, led by the Senate Watergate Committee and the House Judiciary Committee, held hearings to investigate the scandal and gather evidence. The executive branch, led by President Nixon and his administration, tried to limit the investigation and withhold evidence. The judicial branch, led by the Supreme Court, played a critical role in upholding the rule of law by ordering the release of key evidence and ruling that the President was not above the law.

Ultimately, the Watergate scandal led to the resignation of President Nixon, and it served as a powerful reminder of the importance of the separation of powers and the rule of law in ensuring accountability in government.

Marbury v. Madison is a landmark Supreme Court case that established the principle of judicial review, which allows the courts to review the constitutionality of laws and executive actions. In the case, William Marbury, a Justice of the Peace who had been appointed by President John Adams, sued Secretary of State James Madison for failing to deliver his commission.

The Supreme Court, led by Chief Justice John Marshall, ruled that Marbury was entitled to his commission but that the court did not have the power to compel Madison to deliver it. The Court also established the principle of judicial review, which allows the courts to declare laws or executive actions unconstitutional.

The significance of Marbury v. Madison established the principle of judicial review and established the Supreme Court as an equal branch of government with the power to check the other branches.

Overall, the system of checks and balances is designed to ensure that no one branch of government becomes too powerful. By distributing power among the legislative, executive, and judicial branches, the Constitution ensures that each branch has a specific set of powers and responsibilities that are designed to work together to create a balance of power. This system promotes accountability, compromise, and negotiation, and it helps to prevent abuses of power that can threaten individual freedoms and democracy.

By distributing power among the legislative, executive, and judicial branches of government, the Constitution ensures that no one branch can become too powerful and that individual freedoms and rights are protected. The system of checks and balances also promotes accountability, compromise, and negotiation, which are essential components of a healthy democracy. Without checks and balances, the United States government would be much more vulnerable to abuses of power and the erosion of individual freedoms.

CHAPTER 2: INDIVIDUAL RIGHTS PROTECTIONS

The Bill of Rights is a crucial part of the United States Constitution. It consists of the first ten amendments to the Constitution and was ratified on December 15, 1791. The Bill of Rights provides explicit protections for individual liberties, such as freedom of speech, religion, and the press, as well as the right to bear arms, due process of law, and protection against unreasonable searches and seizures. The following is a detailed overview of the Bill of Rights and its significance in protecting individual liberties.

The First Amendment protects the freedom of speech, religion, assembly, and the press. This amendment is critical to the functioning of a democratic society, as it allows individuals to express their views, opinions, and beliefs without fear of government retaliation. The First Amendment also protects the right to petition the government for a redress of grievances, allowing citizens to hold their elected officials accountable.

The First Amendment allows individuals to express their views and opinions without fear of government censorship or retaliation. It ensures that the government cannot restrict or control the press, religious practices, or public assembly. The First Amendment also protects the right to petition the government for redress of grievances.

Freedom of speech is perhaps the most well-known protection offered by the First Amendment. It allows individuals to speak their minds without fear of government censorship or retaliation. This protection extends to all forms of expression, including political speech, artistic expression, and commercial speech. The courts have applied the First Amendment in cases involving freedom of the press, hate speech, and campaign finance.

The First Amendment has been the subject of many important legal battles throughout American history. For example, in the landmark case New York Times Co. v. United States (1971), the Supreme Court held that the government could not prevent the publication of classified information, even if it posed a threat to national security. This case established the principle that the press has a constitutional right to publish information of public interest.

The Second Amendment protects the right to bear arms. This amendment has been the subject of much controversy in recent years, with some arguing that it should be repealed or amended, while others believe it is critical to protecting individual liberties. The Second Amendment has been interpreted by the courts to allow individuals to own firearms for self-defense and hunting, but it does not protect the right to own military-style weapons or other dangerous firearms.

The Second Amendment to the United States Constitution is one of the most controversial and widely debated amendments in the Constitution. It reads, "A well-regulated Militia, being necessary to the security of a free State, the right of the people to keep and bear Arms, shall not be infringed." The Second Amendment has been the subject of countless legal debates and political discussions, and its interpretation remains a source of contention among lawmakers, activists, and citizens.

One of the main reasons the Second Amendment was included in the Bill of Rights was to protect the right of citizens to bear arms for self-defense. In the context of the late 18th century, this right was seen as necessary for individuals to protect themselves, their families, and their property from both criminals and a potentially oppressive government.

Today, the Second Amendment is still viewed by many as a critical protection of the individual's right to self-defense. Supporters of the Second Amendment argue that owning firearms is an essential means of protecting oneself and one's family from potential threats such as home invasion, robbery, or assault. They argue that the right to bear arms is crucial to individual liberty and a free society.

However, the Second Amendment's meaning and interpretation remain hotly contested. Opponents of the Second Amendment argue that the right to bear arms can lead to increased violence and that the government should have more control over firearms ownership to prevent mass shootings and other violent crimes.

Despite the ongoing debates, the Second Amendment remains a vital protection of individual liberty and the right to self-defense. The Supreme Court has upheld an individual's right to keep and bear arms for self-defense in the landmark case District of Columbia v. Heller (2008). In this case, the Court affirmed that the Second Amendment protects an individual's right to own a firearm for lawful purposes, including self-defense.

The Second Amendment also plays a crucial role in protecting the right to bear arms for hunting, recreational shooting, and other lawful activities. It is important to note, however, that the right to bear arms is not an absolute right and is subject to reasonable regulation by the government to protect public safety and prevent harm.

The Third Amendment prohibits the government from quartering soldiers in private homes without the owner's consent. This amendment was added to the Constitution in response to the British practice of quartering troops in private homes during the Revolutionary War. While this amendment is rarely invoked today, it remains a powerful protection of individual property rights.

The Third Amendment to the United States Constitution reads: "No Soldier shall, in time of peace be quartered in any house, without the consent of the Owner, nor in time of war, but in a manner to be prescribed by law." While the Third Amendment is not as widely discussed as other amendments in the Bill of Rights, it remains an essential protection of individual liberties, particularly in the context of modern society.

The Third Amendment was included in the Bill of Rights in response to British colonial practices of quartering troops in private homes during times of war or unrest. The Founders were wary of this practice and sought to ensure that individuals could not be compelled to quarter soldiers in their homes without their consent. Today, the Third Amendment remains an important protection against the government's overreach into private property rights.

While the Third Amendment may not seem relevant in today's society, its principles are still applicable. The amendment serves as a check on the government's power to use private property for its purposes, particularly in the context of military actions. The amendment ensures that individuals have the right to refuse quartering of soldiers in their homes, even during times of war or national emergency.

The Third Amendment is also significant in protecting privacy rights. The amendment recognizes the importance of a person's home as a private space and protects individuals from government intrusion into their homes without consent. In this way, the Third Amendment is a vital protection of individual liberties in a free society.

While the Third Amendment is not as well-known or widely discussed as other amendments in the Bill of Rights, its importance should not be overlooked. The Third Amendment serves as a check on government power, particularly in protecting individual property and privacy rights. The amendment's principles remain relevant in today's society and serve as an essential safeguard of individual liberties.

The Fourth Amendment protects against unreasonable searches and seizures. This amendment requires that law enforcement officials obtain a warrant before searching a person's property or seizing their belongings. The Fourth Amendment is critical to protecting individual privacy rights, as it prevents the government from conducting arbitrary searches or seizures without probable cause.

The Fourth Amendment applies to a wide range of scenarios, including traffic stops, home searches, and digital communications. In recent years, the courts have grappled with how to apply the Fourth Amendment to new technologies, such as cell phones and social media.

The Fourth Amendment has been the subject of many important legal battles throughout American history. For example, in the landmark case Mapp v. Ohio (1961), the Supreme Court held that evidence obtained through an illegal search and seizure could not be used in a criminal trial. This case established the principle that the Fourth Amendment applies to state and local law enforcement agencies, not just the federal government. In another landmark case, United States v. Jones (2012), the Supreme Court held that attaching a GPS device to a suspect's car without a warrant constituted an unreasonable search under the Fourth Amendment. This case established the principle that technology cannot erode the protections offered by the Fourth Amendment.

The Fifth Amendment protects individuals from self-incrimination and double jeopardy. This amendment also requires that individuals be provided with due process of law and just compensation for any property taken by the government. The Fifth Amendment is critical to protecting individual rights in criminal proceedings and in cases where the government is taking private property for public use.

One of the key protections offered by the Fifth Amendment is the right against self-incrimination. This means that individuals cannot be forced to testify against themselves in a criminal trial. The Fifth Amendment protects individuals from being compelled to provide evidence that could be used against them in court. This protection is critical to ensuring that individuals are not coerced into confessing to crimes they did not commit or providing evidence that could be used to wrongly convict them.

The Fifth Amendment also protects individuals from double jeopardy, which means that they cannot be tried twice for the same crime. This protection ensures that individuals are not subject to multiple prosecutions for the same offense, which could lead to harassment and injustice.

Another important protection offered by the Fifth Amendment is the guarantee of due process of law. This means that individuals cannot be deprived of their life, liberty, or property without a fair and just legal process. The Fifth Amendment ensures that individuals have the right to a fair trial, access to legal representation, and a chance to present evidence in their defense. It also prohibits the government from using arbitrary or unfair procedures in legal proceedings.

The Fifth Amendment also provides protections against the government seizing private property without just compensation. This is known as the Takings Clause, and it ensures that individuals are fairly compensated for any property that is taken by the government for public use.

The Sixth Amendment protects the right to a fair and speedy trial, as well as the right to an impartial jury and the right to be informed of the charges against you. The Sixth Amendment is critical to ensuring that individuals are not unfairly prosecuted or punished by the government. The amendment also provides the right to be informed of the charges against oneself, the right to confront witnesses, the right to compel witnesses to testify, and the right to the assistance of counsel. These protections are crucial in ensuring that individuals are not unjustly convicted or punished by the government.

The right to a fair trial is essential to a just society, and the Sixth Amendment guarantees this right to every individual accused of a crime. The amendment ensures that individuals have the right to be heard in a court of law and to defend themselves against accusations of wrongdoing. This right to a fair trial is particularly important in cases where the government has a lot of power, such as cases involving national security or terrorism.

The Sixth Amendment's guarantee of a speedy trial is also important in protecting individual liberties. This provision ensures that individuals are not held in jail indefinitely without trial, as this would be a violation of their constitutional rights. The public trial requirement of the Sixth Amendment ensures that the trial process is transparent and accountable, allowing the public to observe and assess the fairness of the proceedings.

The right to counsel is another crucial protection provided by the Sixth Amendment. The amendment ensures that individuals have the right to legal representation and that they are not forced to represent themselves in court. This right is particularly important for individuals who cannot afford legal representation, as it ensures that they have access to competent legal counsel.

The Sixth Amendment's protections are essential in protecting individual liberties and ensuring that the criminal justice system operates fairly and justly. The amendment provides important protections against government overreach and ensures that individuals are not unjustly accused or punished. In today's society, the Sixth Amendment remains an essential protection of individual liberties and a cornerstone of the American legal system.

The Seventh Amendment guarantees the right to a trial by jury in civil cases. This amendment is critical to protecting individual property rights and ensuring that individuals have access to justice in cases where their rights have been violated.

The Seventh Amendment ensures that individuals have the right to a trial by jury in civil cases where the amount in controversy exceeds $20. This right is essential because it allows individuals to have their disputes resolved by a group of their peers rather than by a judge alone. This provides a check against judicial bias or error and helps ensure that justice is served in civil cases.

The right to a trial by jury is also significant in protecting individual liberties because it provides a level of accountability and transparency in the legal system. Juries are made up of ordinary citizens who are selected randomly, and their decisions are based on the evidence presented in the case. This provides a safeguard against government overreach and ensures that individuals have a say in the outcome of their case.

Furthermore, the Seventh Amendment's protection of the right to a trial by jury is essential in protecting against frivolous lawsuits. If individuals were not guaranteed the right to a trial by jury, it would be much easier for large corporations or wealthy individuals to use the legal system to harass or intimidate their opponents. The Seventh Amendment ensures that cases must be heard by a jury of one's peers, which provides a level of fairness and accountability in the legal system.

While the Seventh Amendment may not seem as significant as some of the other amendments in the Bill of Rights, its principles are still relevant today. The Seventh Amendment ensures that individuals have the right to a fair trial in civil cases, and it serves as a check against government overreach and abuse of power. The amendment's principles remain essential in protecting individual liberties in a free society.

The Eighth Amendment prohibits excessive bail and fines, as well as cruel and unusual punishment. This amendment is critical to protecting individual rights in criminal cases and ensuring that individuals are not subjected to harsh or arbitrary punishment by the government.

One of the key protections of the Eighth Amendment is against cruel and unusual punishment. This means that the government cannot inflict torture or other forms of cruel and degrading treatment on individuals, even those who have been convicted of crimes. This protection is essential in maintaining a just and humane criminal justice system, as it prevents the government from using excessive force or punishment as a means of control or deterrence.

The Eighth Amendment's prohibition on excessive bail and fines also plays an important role in protecting individual liberties. Bail is a mechanism used by the criminal justice system to ensure that individuals show up for trial, but excessive bail can be used as a means of punishing individuals before they have been convicted of a crime. The prohibition on excessive bail ensures that individuals are not punished before they have been found guilty.

Similarly, excessive fines can be used as a means of punishing individuals beyond what is reasonable or necessary. The Eighth Amendment ensures that fines are not excessive, and that they are proportional to the offense committed.

The importance of the Eighth Amendment remains relevant today, as it continues to protect individuals from government abuse of power. The amendment provides critical protections against inhumane treatment, excessive punishment, and financial ruin. The principles of the Eighth Amendment are fundamental to a just and free society, and they serve as a vital safeguard against government overreach and abuse of power.

The Ninth Amendment states that the enumeration of certain rights in the Constitution shall not be construed to deny or disparage other rights retained by the people. This amendment is critical to protecting individual rights that may not be explicitly stated in the Constitution.

The Ninth Amendment is rooted in the idea that individuals have inherent rights that are not granted by the government, but rather exist independently of it. The amendment acknowledges that the Constitution does not provide an exhaustive list of individual rights, and that the people retain other rights that are not specifically mentioned in the Constitution.

The importance of the Ninth Amendment today lies in its role in protecting individual liberties that are not explicitly listed in the Constitution. This includes rights such as privacy, freedom of association, and reproductive rights. The amendment recognizes that the Constitution's enumeration of certain rights should not be interpreted to mean that other fundamental rights do not exist or are not protected.

Furthermore, the Ninth Amendment helps protect against the government's tendency to limit individual rights through the interpretation of the

Constitution. The amendment serves as a safeguard against government encroachment on individual liberties by affirming that the Constitution protects a broad range of rights beyond those listed in the Bill of Rights.

In recent years, the Ninth Amendment has been invoked in legal challenges to government actions that are seen as infringing on individual rights. For example, the Supreme Court's landmark decision in Roe v. Wade relied on the Ninth Amendment in its recognition of a woman's right to choose whether to have an abortion.

The Tenth Amendment reserves powers not delegated to the federal government to the states or to the people. This amendment is critical to protecting state sovereignty and ensuring that the federal government does not overreach its authority.

The Tenth Amendment is rooted in the idea of federalism, which is the system of government in which power is divided between a central authority (in this case, the federal government) and constituent political units (in this case, the states). The Tenth Amendment affirms that the Constitution grants limited and enumerated powers to the federal government, and that all other powers are reserved to the states or to the people.

The importance of the Tenth Amendment today lies in its role in protecting state sovereignty and promoting decentralization of power. The amendment helps ensure that the federal government does not encroach on the powers and responsibilities of state governments, and that states are free to make decisions that are best suited to their particular circumstances.

The Tenth Amendment has been invoked in a wide range of legal and political debates, including issues related to healthcare, drug policy, gun control, and immigration. For example, some states have asserted their right to legalize marijuana despite federal laws prohibiting its use, citing the Tenth Amendment as support for their actions.

Furthermore, the Tenth Amendment helps promote a more responsive and accountable government by allowing states to experiment with different policies and approaches. This diversity of policy experimentation allows for greater innovation and adaptation to changing circumstances, and it provides a mechanism for states to respond to the unique needs and preferences of their citizens.

The Tenth Amendment remains relevant today as a critical protection of state sovereignty and a safeguard against the concentration of power in the federal government. The amendment affirms the importance of limited and decentralized government, and it helps promote a more responsive and accountable system of governance.

CHAPTER 3: FLEXIBILITY IN FUTURE GENERATIONS

The Constitution of the United States is often referred to as a living document because of its ability to adapt and change with the times. This flexibility is a result of several provisions built into the Constitution itself, as well as the ability of the branches of government and the people to interpret and amend the document.

One of the key ways that the Constitution adapts to changing times is through interpretation by the judicial branch. The Constitution is a broad framework of principles and values, and its interpretation can evolve over time as new social, political, and economic conditions arise. For example, the Supreme Court's landmark decision in Brown v. Board of Education (1954) declared segregation in public schools to be unconstitutional, overturning the previous "separate but equal" doctrine established by Plessy v. Ferguson (1896). This interpretation reflected changing attitudes towards race and equality in American society and helped to move the country towards greater civil rights and social justice.

Another way the Constitution adapts to changing times is through the amendment process. The Constitution has been amended 27 times since its ratification in 1788, reflecting changing values, social norms, and political circumstances. For example, the 13th, 14th, and 15th Amendments, ratified in the aftermath of the Civil War, abolished slavery, granted citizenship and equal protection under the law to all persons born or naturalized in the United States, and prohibited racial discrimination in voting. Similarly, the 19th Amendment, ratified in 1920, granted women the right to vote, reflecting changing attitudes towards gender equality.

In addition to interpretation and amendment, the Constitution also adapts to changing times through the exercise of the various powers granted to the branches of government. For example, the Commerce Clause of the Constitution (Article I, Section 8) has been interpreted to allow the federal government to regulate a wide range of economic activities, from interstate commerce to labor laws to environmental regulations. Similarly, the Necessary and Proper Clause (Article I, Section 8) gives Congress the power to enact laws that are necessary and proper to carry out its other powers and duties, providing flexibility in addressing new challenges and circumstances.

Finally, the Constitution adapts to changing times through the participation of the people. The Constitution is designed to be a democratic document, and the people have the power to shape its interpretation and implementation through elections, advocacy, and activism. For example, the Civil Rights Movement of the 1950s and 1960s, led by figures such as Martin Luther King Jr., used nonviolent protest and civil disobedience to draw attention to the injustices of racial segregation and discrimination. Their efforts helped to shift public opinion and political will, leading to changes in laws and policies that reflected a more inclusive and just society.

The United States Constitution is a foundational document that outlines the structure and powers of the federal government, as well as the rights and freedoms of the American people. Although the Constitution has been amended only 27 times since its ratification in 1788, the amendment process is an important part of the document's adaptability and longevity.

The process for amending the Constitution is set forth in Article V, which outlines the two-step process for making changes to the document. The first step is the proposal of an amendment, which can be initiated by either Congress or a convention called for this purpose by two-thirds of the state legislatures.

The more common method of proposing an amendment is by a two-thirds vote of both the Senate and the House of Representatives. This method has been used for all but one of the 27 amendments to the Constitution. The proposed amendment must then be sent to the states for ratification.

The second step in the amendment process is ratification. This can be done by either three-fourths of the state legislatures or conventions held in three-fourths of the states. The more common method of ratification is by the state legislatures, which has been used for all but one of the 27 amendments.

The purpose of the amendment process is to allow the Constitution to adapt to changing circumstances and societal values. The framers of the Constitution recognized that the document was not perfect and that it would need to change over time. They also recognized that the process of amending the Constitution should not be too easy, as this could lead to changes that were not carefully considered or broadly supported.

The amendment process is deliberately difficult, requiring significant support from both Congress and the states in order to make changes to the Constitution. This ensures that amendments are made only after careful consideration and broad consensus, and that they reflect the values and aspirations of the American people.

The United States Constitution is intentionally difficult to amend because the framers wanted to ensure that changes to the document would not be made too easily or too quickly. There were several reasons why the framers made the amendment process difficult:

1. **Protecting the document's integrity:** The Constitution is the foundational document that outlines the structure and powers of the

federal government, as well as the rights and freedoms of the American people. The framers recognized that any changes to the document could have significant consequences, and they wanted to ensure that the Constitution remained a stable and enduring document.

2. **Ensuring careful consideration:** The framers recognized that the amendment process should not be too easy, as this could lead to changes that were not carefully considered or broadly supported. They believed that amendments should only be made after significant debate and discussion, and that they should reflect the values and aspirations of the American people.

3. **Protecting against tyranny of the majority:** The framers were concerned that a simple majority could easily amend the Constitution to the detriment of minority groups or individual rights. By requiring

significant support from both Congress and the states, the amendment process ensures that amendments are made only after careful consideration and broad consensus.

4. **Preserving federalism:** The framers recognized that the states played a critical role in the federal system of government, and they wanted to ensure that any changes to the Constitution would require the support of the states. By requiring three-fourths of the states to ratify an amendment, the amendment process ensures that the states have a significant say in any changes to the document.

The difficulty of amending the Constitution is an intentional feature of the document, designed to ensure that any changes are made thoughtfully and with broad support. While the amendment process can be frustratingly slow at times, it is a critical aspect of the Constitution's adaptability and longevity, ensuring that the document remains relevant and effective in a changing world.

There have been 27 amendments to the United States Constitution, each with its own historical context and significance. Here are a few examples:

1. **19th Amendment:** This amendment, ratified in 1920, granted women the right to vote. It was the culmination of decades of activism by suffragists who fought for women's political rights. Today, the 19th Amendment remains a symbol of progress and equality, and its principles continue to inspire movements for women's empowerment around the world.

2. **26th Amendment:** This amendment, ratified in 1971, lowered the voting age to 18. The Vietnam War was a major catalyst for the amendment, as many young Americans were being drafted into military service without the right to vote. Today, the

26th Amendment remains relevant as young people continue to push for greater representation in government and politics.

3. **13th Amendment:** This amendment, ratified in 1865, abolished slavery and involuntary servitude in the United States. It was a major milestone in the struggle for civil rights and represented a critical turning point in American history. Today, the 13th Amendment remains a testament to the enduring power of individual freedom and the importance of standing up for what is right.

4. **14th Amendment:** This amendment, ratified in 1868, established equal protection under the law and due process of law for all citizens, regardless of race or ethnicity. It was a critical step in the fight for civil rights, and its principles continue to be invoked in legal battles over discrimination and inequality today.

5. **21st Amendment:** This amendment, ratified in 1933, repealed Prohibition and ended the era of alcohol prohibition in the United States. While Prohibition was a failed experiment, the 21st Amendment remains relevant today as a reminder of the importance of individual freedoms and the dangers of government overreach.

These amendments continue to have important applications today. The 19th Amendment has paved the way for greater gender equality and representation in government and politics, while the 26th Amendment ensures that young people have a voice in shaping the future of the country.

The 13th and 14th Amendments have helped to establish civil rights and equal protection under the law, while the 21st Amendment serves as a reminder of the importance of individual freedoms and the dangers of government overreach. Together, these amendments reflect the ongoing struggle for justice, equality, and freedom in the United States, and they continue to inspire individuals and movements around the world.

The United States Constitution was written to establish the framework of the new nation's government. Over time, however, societal values and norms evolved, leading to the need for the Constitution to adapt to changing times.

One reason why the adaptability of the Constitution is so important is that it must reflect changing societal values and norms. This is because as society changes, so too do the values and norms that govern it.

For example, the Constitution has had to adapt to changing public opinion on issues such as civil rights, same-sex marriage, and gun control. The Constitution must be able to keep up with these changes and adapt accordingly.

Another reason why adaptability is crucial is that emerging issues may arise that were not foreseen by the Constitution's original authors. For example, the Constitution does not mention the internet or social media, yet these platforms have had a significant impact on society and the way we communicate. As a result, there may be a need to adapt the Constitution to address new issues that arise.

Ultimately, the adaptability of the Constitution is crucial because it ensures that the document remains relevant and effective in governing the nation. By adapting to changing times and emerging issues, the Constitution can continue to serve as the foundation of the government and provide a framework for a just and prosperous society.

CHAPTER 4: CHALLENGES TO THE CONSTITUTION

The United States Constitution, since its inception in 1787, has faced numerous challenges throughout American history. The Constitution was created to establish a framework for the new nation's government, but over time, it has had to adapt to changing times, societal values, and emerging issues. Some of the significant challenges the Constitution has faced include slavery, the balance of power between the federal and state governments, civil rights, and the changing nature of the economy.

One of the earliest and most significant challenges faced by the Constitution was the issue of slavery. The Constitution was drafted in a time when slavery was legal and widespread in the United States. The issue of slavery caused significant tensions between the northern and southern states, ultimately leading to the Civil War. The Constitution did not directly address the issue of slavery, and it was not until the 13th Amendment was ratified in 1865 that slavery was officially abolished in the United States.

Another significant challenge faced by the Constitution was the balance of power between the federal and state governments. This issue was central to the debates that took place during the drafting of the Constitution and has continued to be a source of tension throughout American history.

The Constitution established a system of federalism, which divided powers between the federal government and the states. However, the balance of power between the two levels of government has been a subject of ongoing debate and has been tested by events such as the Civil War, the New Deal, and the Civil Rights Movement.

During the Civil War, the balance of power between the federal and state governments was tested as southern states seceded from the Union. The federal government ultimately prevailed, and the Civil War cemented the federal government's supremacy over the states. However, debates over federal power continued, and the New Deal era marked a significant expansion of federal power. The Civil Rights Movement also saw federal power used to enforce civil rights laws in the face of opposition from some states.

Civil rights have been another significant challenge faced by the Constitution throughout American history. The Constitution was written in a time when many of the rights we take for granted today, such as freedom of speech and religion, were not explicitly protected. The Constitution also did not address issues such as voting rights and equal protection under the law. As a result, civil rights have been a source of ongoing struggle throughout American history.

The Civil War led to the abolition of slavery, but it was not until the Civil Rights Movement of the 1960s that significant progress was made in protecting the civil rights of African Americans. The Civil Rights Act of 1964 and the Voting Rights Act of 1965 were significant milestones in the fight for civil rights, but the struggle continues to this day. Other marginalized groups, such as women, LGBTQ+ individuals, and people with disabilities, have also fought for and continue to fight for their civil rights.

The changing nature of the economy has also presented challenges for the Constitution. The Constitution was written in a time when the economy was primarily based on agriculture and small-scale industry. However, the Industrial Revolution and the rise of big business transformed the economy, creating new challenges for the Constitution.

The Constitution did not anticipate the rise of large corporations, which can wield significant economic and political power. The concentration of wealth and power in the hands of a few has led to concerns about the fairness of the economic system and the influence of money in politics. The Constitution has been amended to address some of these concerns, such as the 17th Amendment, which established the direct election of Senators, and the 19th Amendment, which gave women the right to vote.

The Constitution has also faced challenges related to individual rights and civil liberties. The Constitution includes the Bill of Rights, which guarantees certain rights to citizens, such as freedom of speech, religion, and the press. However, throughout American history, these rights have been tested and challenged.

One of the most significant challenges to individual rights was the internment of Japanese

Americans during World War II. The government argued that the internment was necessary for national security, but it was ultimately found to be unconstitutional. More recently, there have been debates over issues such as government surveillance, hate speech, and the rights of protesters.

Despite its enduring popularity, the Constitution has faced numerous challenges over the years, particularly in the areas of civil liberties and executive power. In this essay, we will explore some of these contemporary challenges, including the ongoing debates over the Second Amendment and the scope of executive power.

The Second Amendment to the United States Constitution protects the right of citizens to keep and bear arms. This amendment has been the subject of much debate in recent years, particularly in the wake of mass shootings and other acts of gun violence. On one side of the debate are those who argue that the Second Amendment protects an individual's right to own firearms for self-defense, hunting, and other lawful purposes. They contend that any attempt to restrict access to guns would violate this right and would be an infringement on individual liberties.

On the other side of the debate are those who argue that the Second Amendment was never intended to be an unlimited right to own firearms. They point to the fact that the amendment's language includes the phrase "well-regulated militia," suggesting that the right to bear arms was meant to be limited to those who are part of a regulated military organization. They also argue that the amendment was written in a historical context in which guns were much less powerful than they are today and that the risks associated with widespread gun ownership have increased dramatically in modern times.

The debate over the Second Amendment is likely to continue for some time, as both sides have passionate supporters who are committed to their respective positions. However, it is important to note that the Supreme Court has already weighed in on this issue, with a landmark decision in 2008 (District of Columbia v. Heller) upholding an individual's right to own firearms for self-defense. Nevertheless, states and municipalities continue to pass laws restricting access to firearms, prompting legal challenges that will likely continue to be litigated in the courts.

Another contemporary challenge to the Constitution concerns the scope of executive power. The Constitution divides power between three branches of government—the legislative, executive, and judicial—with each branch having its own set of checks and balances to prevent any one branch from becoming too powerful. However, in recent years, there has been concern that the executive branch has been asserting more power than it is entitled to under the Constitution.

One example of this is the use of executive orders. Executive orders are directives issued by the President that have the force of law. While they have been used throughout American history, some argue that recent Presidents have been using them more frequently and in more expansive ways than their predecessors. Critics contend that this undermines the separation of powers between the executive and legislative branches, as executive orders can be used to bypass the legislative process.

Another example of executive power concerns the use of emergency powers. The Constitution grants the President certain emergency powers, such as the power to declare martial law or to suspend the writ of habeas corpus in times of national crisis. However, there is concern that these emergency powers have been abused in recent years, particularly in the context of the so-called "War on Terror." Critics argue that the executive branch has used these emergency powers to justify actions that violate civil liberties and the rule of law, such as the use of torture, indefinite detention, and warrantless surveillance.

The right to vote is essential to American democracy. However, in recent years, there have been challenges to voting rights in the United States. One major issue is voter suppression, which takes many forms. Some states have passed laws that require voters to present government-issued photo identification, which can disproportionately affect low-income and minority voters who are less likely to have such identification. Other forms of voter suppression include limiting early voting, closing polling places in certain areas, and purging voter rolls.

Another challenge to voting rights is gerrymandering, the practice of redrawing electoral districts to benefit one political party or group. Gerrymandering can make it difficult for certain groups to have their voices heard and can result in uncompetitive elections that do not reflect the will of the people.

The Constitution grants Congress the power to regulate immigration, but in recent years, there have been significant challenges to the government's ability to enforce immigration laws. One of the biggest challenges is the ongoing debate over Deferred Action for Childhood Arrivals (DACA). This program, created by executive order under President Obama, allows certain undocumented immigrants who came to the United States as children to receive temporary protection from deportation and work authorization. However, the Trump administration attempted to rescind the program in 2017, leading to legal challenges that are ongoing.

Another challenge to immigration policy concerns the treatment of immigrants at the southern border. The Trump administration's "zero tolerance" policy, which resulted in the separation of families at the border, was widely criticized as inhumane and unconstitutional. The Biden administration has since taken steps to reverse this policy, but the issue of immigration remains a divisive one in American politics.

The role of money in politics has been a significant challenge to the Constitution in recent years. The Supreme Court's decision in Citizens United v. FEC in 2010 allowed corporations and unions to spend unlimited amounts of money on political campaigns, leading to a flood of "dark money" in American politics. This has raised concerns about the influence of wealthy donors and corporations on the political process, and the impact of money on democracy itself.

The ongoing debates over voting rights, immigration, and the role of money in politics reflect the dynamic nature of American democracy. While these challenges are significant, they also offer opportunities for progress and reform. By engaging in civil discourse and working together, Americans can ensure that the Constitution continues to serve as a foundation for a fair and just society.

One of the earliest challenges to the Constitution was the debate over the scope of executive power. This issue was particularly relevant during the presidency of George Washington, who set many precedents for the office. Washington's use of executive power was controversial, and some argued that it exceeded the bounds of the Constitution. However, Washington's actions helped to establish the precedent of a strong executive branch that has endured to this day.

Another significant challenge to the Constitution was the Civil War. The conflict raised questions about the relationship between the federal government and the states, as well as the balance of power between the branches of government. The aftermath of the war led to a series of constitutional amendments, including the 13th, 14th, and 15th Amendments, which abolished slavery, granted citizenship to former slaves, and extended voting rights to African American men.

More recent challenges to the Constitution include debates over civil rights, voting rights, and the role of money in politics. These challenges have resulted in landmark Supreme Court decisions, such as Brown v. The Board of Education, which struck down segregation in public institutions, and have shown a need to continue to adapt to meet these challenges. One issue that is likely to be a significant challenge in the coming years is climate change. The Constitution does not explicitly address this issue, but it may need to be reinterpreted to allow for a more robust response to the threat of climate change. This could include changes to the Commerce Clause, which gives Congress the power to regulate commerce among the states, or the Due Process Clause, which guarantees equal protection under the law.

Another challenge that the Constitution may need to adapt to is the rise of technology. The Constitution was written in an era before the internet, social media, and other digital technologies existed. As these technologies continue to evolve, they raise new questions about privacy, free speech, and government surveillance. The Constitution may need to be reinterpreted to ensure that it continues to protect the rights of citizens in the digital age.

The United States Constitution has faced numerous challenges throughout its history, but it has remained a foundation of American governance.

The Constitution has adapted to meet past challenges, including debates over the scope of executive power, the Civil War, and civil rights. As the United States faces new challenges in the 21st century, such as climate change and the rise of technology, the Constitution will need to continue to adapt to ensure that schools, and Citizens United v. FEC, which allows corporations and unions to spend unlimited amounts of money on political campaigns. These decisions have shaped the legal landscape of the United States and helped to define the boundaries of American democracy.

As the United States faces new challenges in the 21st century, the Conit remains a relevant and effective document for future generations.

CHAPTER 5: INDIVIDUAL RIGHTS

Individual rights refer to a set of moral principles and legal entitlements that individuals possess, which are aimed at ensuring their freedom, autonomy, and dignity in society. These rights include civil rights, political rights, and social rights, which are protected by the law and enforceable against any violation. The concept of individual rights has a rich and complex history that spans across different cultures, civilizations, and eras. This paper provides a definition of individual rights and a brief history of the concept, highlighting its evolution and significance in different contexts.

Individual rights are moral and legal entitlements that individuals possess by virtue of their humanity or citizenship, which are aimed at promoting their well-being, freedom, autonomy, and dignity in society. These rights are inherent, inalienable, and universal, meaning that they are not granted by the state or any other authority, but rather, they are derived from the natural law or the social contract between individuals and the state. Individual rights include civil rights, which protect individuals from discrimination, oppression, and abuse by the state or other individuals; political rights, which empower individuals to participate in the governance of their society, such as the right to vote, run for office, and free speech; and social rights, which ensure that individuals have access to basic necessities of life, such as education, healthcare, housing, and food.

The concept of individual rights has a long and complex history that dates back to ancient civilizations, such as Greece, Rome, and Egypt. In these societies, individual rights were closely tied to the notion of citizenship, which was restricted to a privileged class of men who were entitled to political participation and legal protection. For instance, in ancient Athens, only male citizens who were free, born in Athens, and over 18 years of age had the right to vote, speak in public, and hold public office. Women, slaves, foreigners, and children were excluded from these rights and treated as inferior beings.

During the Middle Ages, the concept of individual rights was largely overshadowed by the dominance of religious and feudal authorities, which upheld the idea of divine right and hierarchy. However, with the rise of the Renaissance, the Reformation, and the Enlightenment in Europe, the concept of individual rights regained prominence as a counterforce to the authoritarianism of the Church and the state. The Renaissance humanists, such as Francesco Petrarch and Leonardo da Vinci, emphasized the value of humanism, reason, and individualism, and called for the revival of classical culture and knowledge. The Reformation leaders, such as Martin Luther and John Calvin, challenged the authority of the Catholic Church and advocated for the individual's right to interpret the Bible and worship God freely. The Enlightenment philosophers, such as John Locke, Jean-Jacques Rousseau, and Immanuel Kant, developed a secular and rationalist view of human nature and society, and argued that individuals possess natural rights that precede and limit the power of the state.

The concept of individual rights became a central theme of the American Revolution and the French Revolution, which were inspired by the Enlightenment ideas of liberty, equality, and democracy. In the United States, the Declaration of Independence, adopted in 1776, proclaimed that "all men are created equal, that they are endowed by their Creator with certain unalienable Rights, that among these are Life, Liberty and the pursuit of Happiness." This statement enshrined the concept of natural rights as the foundation of American democracy and provided the moral and legal basis for the American Bill of Rights, which was added to the Constitution in 1791 and guaranteed individual freedoms, such as freedom of speech, religion, and assembly, and due process of law.

John Locke, in particular, was a major influence on the development of the concept of individual rights. He argued that all individuals had a natural right to life, liberty, and property, and that the purpose of government was to protect these rights. He believed that these rights were inherent in human nature and were not granted by any authority.

The concept of individual rights was also central to the American Revolution, which was fought in the late 18th century. The Declaration of Independence, which was drafted by Thomas Jefferson, declared that all men were created equal and that they had certain inalienable rights, including the right to life, liberty, and the pursuit of happiness.

In the aftermath of the American Revolution, the concept of individual rights became increasingly important in the United States. The Bill of Rights, which was added to the U.S. Constitution in 1791, included a number of individual rights, such as the right to free speech, freedom of religion, and the right to bear arms.

In the 19th century, the concept of individual rights continued to evolve. The abolitionist movement, which sought to end slavery, was based on the belief that all individuals had a natural right to freedom. The women's suffrage movement, which sought to give women the right to vote, was based on the belief that women had a natural right to political participation.

Individual rights are an essential component of modern society, serving as a foundation for democratic values, social justice, and personal autonomy. These rights are a reflection of the basic human dignity and equality that we all share, and they empower individuals to assert their interests and beliefs without fear of repression or persecution. In this paper, I will argue that individual rights matter in the modern world because they promote freedom, diversity, and social progress.

Firstly, individual rights promote freedom by ensuring that individuals have the ability to make their own choices and live according to their own values. Without individual rights, individuals would be subject to the arbitrary will of those in power, unable to exercise their own agency or live according to their own conscience. The right to free speech, for example, allows individuals to express their opinions and engage in political discourse without fear of retaliation or censorship. This right is particularly important in the modern world, where the spread of information and ideas through social media and other platforms has led to increased political engagement and awareness.

Similarly, individual rights protect freedom of religion, allowing individuals to practice their own beliefs and worship in their own way. This right is particularly important in a world that is increasingly diverse and multicultural, as it allows individuals to maintain their own cultural identity and beliefs without fear of discrimination or persecution. The right to freedom of assembly and association also allows individuals to come together to advocate for their interests and beliefs, promoting social and political change and allowing individuals to work towards shared goals and values.

In addition, individual rights matter because they promote human dignity. Human beings have inherent dignity simply by virtue of being human, and this dignity must be respected and protected.

The recognition and protection of individual rights are essential for upholding human dignity and ensuring that individuals are treated with respect and fairness.

Individual rights matter because they promote social justice. In many cases, individuals who are marginalized or oppressed have their rights violated by those who hold power. The recognition and protection of individual rights are essential for ensuring that individuals who are marginalized or oppressed have their rights protected and their dignity upheld. In this way, individual rights play an important role in promoting social justice and advancing the cause of human rights.

In the modern world, individual rights face a number of challenges. The growth of new technologies, the rise of global corporations, and the increasing power of governments all present challenges to the recognition and protection of individual rights. It is therefore important to continue to promote the recognition and protection of individual rights in order to ensure that individuals are able to live with dignity, autonomy, and freedom in a rapidly changing world.

CHAPTER 6: PHILOSOPHICAL BASIS FOR INDIVIDUAL RIGHTS

Individual rights refer to the inherent rights that each person is entitled to by virtue of their existence. These rights are often considered fundamental to human dignity and freedom, and they are typically protected by legal systems and governments. Philosophical arguments for individual rights have been a central theme in political philosophy for centuries. This essay provides an overview of different philosophical arguments for individual rights, exploring their history, development, and applications.

The natural rights theory is perhaps the most well-known and influential argument for individual rights. According to this theory, human beings possess inherent, natural rights that are not dependent on any external authority or social contract. These rights are grounded in human nature and are therefore universal and inalienable.

Examples of natural rights include the right to life, liberty, and property.

The natural rights theory can be traced back to ancient Greek philosophy, but it gained prominence during the Enlightenment period in the 17th and 18th centuries. The English philosopher John Locke is often credited with developing the natural rights theory. He argued that individuals have a right to life, liberty, and property, and that these rights are protected by a social contract between the people and their government. The American Declaration of Independence also reflects the natural rights theory, with its famous phrase "life, liberty, and the pursuit of happiness" as unalienable rights.

Critics of the natural rights theory argue that the concept of inherent, natural rights is a fiction that has no basis in reality. They argue that rights are not innate, but rather are created and protected by social institutions and legal systems. Additionally, some argue that the natural rights theory does not provide a clear way to resolve conflicts between different rights claims or to balance individual rights against the needs of society as a whole.

Utilitarianism is a philosophical approach that seeks to promote the greatest happiness for the greatest number of people. This approach holds that actions should be evaluated based on their ability to produce positive outcomes for the largest possible group of people. Utilitarianism is often seen as incompatible with individual rights, since the interests of the individual may sometimes conflict with the interests of the majority.

However, some utilitarian philosophers argue that individual rights are necessary for the greatest happiness of society as a whole. They argue that individual rights protect people from harm and exploitation, and that this protection is necessary for a just and equitable society. For example, the utilitarian philosopher John Stuart Mill argued that individual rights are essential for the development of human potential and creativity, which in turn contribute to the overall well-being of society.

Critics of utilitarianism argue that the approach is too focused on the aggregate happiness of society and does not take into account the dignity and autonomy of individual persons. They argue that utilitarianism can be used to justify actions that violate individual rights, as long as the overall happiness of society is increased. They argue that individual rights protect people from harm and exploitation, and that this protection is necessary for a just and equitable society. For example, the utilitarian philosopher John Stuart Mill argued that individual rights are essential for the development of human potential and creativity, which in turn contribute to the overall well-being of society.

Social contract theory is a political philosophy that seeks to explain the origins of government and the rights and duties of citizens. According to this theory, individuals voluntarily give up some of their rights and freedoms in exchange for the protection and security provided by a government. The social contract is an agreement between the people and their government that establishes the framework for political and social life.

Social contract theorists argue that individual rights are not inherent or natural, but rather are created and protected by the social contract. The rights that individuals possess are those that have been agreed upon in the social contract, and they are subject to change based on the needs and desires of society.

Kantianism is a philosophical approach that is based on the work of the German philosopher Immanuel Kant. According to Kant, individuals have inherent dignity and worth that must be respected by others. Kantianism emphasizes the importance of moral principles and the duty of individuals to respect the rights of others. Kantian ethics are based on the idea of the categorical imperative, which states that individuals should always act in a way that treats others as ends in themselves, rather than as means to an end.

One of the strengths of Kantianism is its emphasis on the inherent dignity and worth of every individual. This approach provides a strong basis for individual rights, as well as for the idea of equal treatment under the law. Additionally, Kantianism provides a clear and objective basis for moral decision-making, based on the principle of treating others as ends in themselves.

However, Kantianism also has some weaknesses. Critics of the approach argue that it can be overly formalistic and rule-bound, and that it does not provide a clear way to resolve conflicts between different moral principles. Additionally, some argue that Kantianism does not provide a clear basis for promoting social justice or addressing structural inequalities in society.

Rawlsianism is a philosophical approach that is based on the work of the American philosopher John Rawls. Rawlsianism emphasizes the importance of social justice and the role of government in promoting a just and equitable society. According to Rawls, a just society is one in which everyone has equal basic rights and opportunities, and in which social and economic inequalities are arranged so as to benefit the least advantaged members of society.

One of the strengths of Rawlsianism is its focus on social justice and the importance of promoting a fair and equitable society. Rawlsianism provides a clear and comprehensive framework for addressing structural inequalities, and it emphasizes the importance of government intervention in promoting social justice. Additionally, Rawlsianism provides a clear basis for evaluating social and economic policies, based on the principle of maximizing the well-being of the least advantaged members of society.

However, Rawlsianism also has some weaknesses. Critics of the approach argue that it is overly idealistic and unrealistic, and that it does not provide a clear way to balance the competing interests of different groups in society. Additionally, some argue that Rawlsianism can be too focused on redistribution and not enough on the importance of individual rights and freedoms.

Kantianism and Rawlsianism share some similarities, such as an emphasis on individual rights, the importance of treating individuals with dignity and respect, and the rejection of utilitarianism as a basis for moral decision-making. However, there are also important differences between the two approaches.

One of the main differences between Kantianism and Rawlsianism is their approach to the role of

government in promoting social justice.
Kantianism emphasizes the importance of individual rights and freedoms, and it does not provide a clear basis for government intervention in promoting social justice. Rawlsianism, on the other hand, places a strong emphasis on the role of government in promoting social justice, and it provides a clear framework for evaluating social and economic policies.

One of the main differences between Kantianism and Rawlsianism is their approach to the role of government in promoting social justice. Kantianism emphasizes individual autonomy and freedom, and therefore, the role of the government is limited to protecting individual rights and ensuring that everyone has an equal opportunity to exercise their freedoms. Kantianism believes that individual rights are inviolable, and the government should not interfere in the exercise of those rights.

On the other hand, Rawlsianism places a strong emphasis on the role of the government in promoting social justice and ensuring that everyone has equal access to resources and opportunities. Rawlsianism argues that in order to achieve social justice, the government must actively intervene in the economy and redistribute resources to benefit the least advantaged members of society.

Rawlsianism believes that government policies must be designed to ensure that every individual has access to the basic necessities of life, including healthcare, education, and housing, and that these policies should be implemented through democratic processes.

Another key difference between Kantianism and Rawlsianism is their approach to individual autonomy. Kantianism places a high value on individual autonomy and believes that individuals have the right to make their own choices and determine their own paths in life. Kantianism argues that individuals have the capacity for rational decision-making and should be allowed to exercise their freedom to pursue their own goals, as long as they do not infringe on the rights of others.

In contrast, Rawlsianism places a stronger emphasis on the social context in which individuals live and argues that individual autonomy can only be achieved when everyone has equal access to resources and opportunities.

Rawlsianism recognizes that social and economic inequalities can limit individual autonomy and agency, and therefore, the government must take active measures to reduce these inequalities and promote equal opportunity.

Chapter 7: Individual Rights and Democracy

Individual rights are essential for protecting the liberty and dignity of each person in a democratic society. These rights are necessary for ensuring that individuals are free to pursue their own goals, make their own choices, and express their own ideas without fear of persecution or discrimination. Individual rights provide a framework for protecting individuals from the power of the government and other individuals.

Individual rights are also important for ensuring that democratic societies are based on the principles of equality and justice. In a democratic society, each individual has an equal right to participate in the political process, to have access to education and healthcare, and to be free from discrimination based on race, gender, religion, or other personal characteristics. Individual rights are essential for ensuring that these principles are upheld and that democratic societies are able to function effectively.

Individual rights are protected by the government in a democratic society. The government is responsible for creating laws and regulations that protect individual rights and for enforcing those laws. The government is also responsible for ensuring that individuals have access to resources and services that enable them to exercise their rights, such as education, healthcare, and legal representation.

However, the government's role in protecting individual rights can sometimes come into conflict with the government's other responsibilities, such as maintaining national security or promoting the common good. In these cases, the government may need to balance individual rights against other societal interests. For example, the government may need to limit an individual's right to free speech if that speech poses a threat to public safety or if it incites violence or hate speech.

Individual rights are not absolute, and there are limits to how far individuals can exercise their rights. These limits are necessary for ensuring that individual rights do not infringe on the rights of others or harm society as a whole. For example, an individual's right to free speech does not extend to hate speech or speech that incites violence. Similarly, an individual's right to bear arms does not extend to the possession of weapons that are considered too dangerous or destructive.

The government is responsible for setting these limits and ensuring that individual rights do not cause harm to others. In some cases, the government may need to restrict individual rights in order to protect the greater good of society. For example, during a pandemic, the government may need to limit the right to free assembly in order to prevent the spread of the virus.

Individual rights can sometimes conflict with each other, leading to difficult ethical and legal dilemmas. For example, an individual's right to free speech may conflict with another individual's right to privacy or freedom from discrimination. In these cases, the government may need to intervene to resolve the conflict and protect the rights of all individuals involved.

Resolving conflicts between individual rights can be challenging, as there is no clear hierarchy of rights. Different societies and cultures may prioritize different rights, and there may be disagreement over which rights should be given precedence in a given situation. In these cases, it is important for the government to take a balanced and nuanced approach that takes into account the needs and perspectives of all individuals involved.

Individual rights are a crucial component of democratic societies as they protect individuals from the tyranny of the majority. The tyranny of the majority occurs when the majority in a democratic society use their power to oppress and marginalize minority groups. In this essay, we will discuss how individual rights protect against the tyranny of the majority, including the importance of individual rights in preventing tyranny, the historical context of individual rights, and examples of how individual rights have been used to protect against tyranny.

Individual rights are essential for preventing tyranny in a democratic society. Without individual rights, the majority in a democratic society could use their power to oppress and marginalize minority groups, leading to an authoritarian government. Individual rights ensure that each person has the right to express their own opinions, beliefs, and values without fear of persecution or discrimination. This protects against the tyranny of the majority by ensuring that each person has an equal voice in the political process and is protected from discrimination and oppression.

Individual rights also protect against the tyranny of the majority by ensuring that the government is accountable to the people. In a democratic society, the government is responsible for protecting the rights and freedoms of all individuals, not just the majority. Individual rights provide a framework for holding the government accountable for its actions and ensuring that it is acting in the best interests of all citizens, not just the majority.

Individual rights are a crucial component of democratic societies as they protect individuals from the tyranny of the majority. The tyranny of the majority occurs when the majority in a democratic society use their power to oppress and marginalize minority groups. In this essay, we will discuss how individual rights protect against the tyranny of the majority, including the importance of individual rights in preventing tyranny, the historical context of individual rights, and examples of how individual rights have been used to protect against tyranny.

Individual rights are essential for preventing tyranny in a democratic society. Without individual rights, the majority in a democratic society could use their power to oppress and marginalize minority groups, leading to an authoritarian government. Individual rights ensure that each person has the right to express their own opinions, beliefs, and values without fear of persecution or discrimination. This protects against the tyranny of the majority by ensuring that each person has an equal voice in the political process and is protected from discrimination and oppression.

Individual rights also protect against the tyranny of the majority by ensuring that the government is accountable to the people. In a democratic society, the government is responsible for protecting the rights and freedoms of all individuals, not just the majority. Individual rights provide a framework for holding the government accountable for its actions and ensuring that it is acting in the best interests of all citizens, not just the majority.

Individual rights have a long and complex history, with different societies and cultures prioritizing different rights at different times. The concept of individual rights can be traced back to ancient Greece and Rome, where individuals had certain rights that were protected by law. However, it was not until the Enlightenment period in the 17th and 18th centuries that the concept of individual rights became more widely recognized.

During the Enlightenment period, philosophers such as John Locke and Jean-Jacques Rousseau argued that individuals had certain natural rights, such as the right to life, liberty, and property. These natural rights were seen as universal and inherent to all individuals, regardless of their social status or position in society. The idea of individual rights was further developed during the American and French Revolutions, where the concept of individual rights was enshrined in the founding documents of these nations.

During the 1960s, African Americans in the United States faced discrimination and oppression from the majority white population. The Civil Rights Movement, led by figures such as Martin Luther King Jr., used the concept of individual rights to fight against this oppression. By invoking their rights to free speech, assembly, and equal protection under the law, African Americans were able to challenge the laws and practices that discriminated against them and demand equal treatment under the law.

The Women's Suffrage Movement in the early 20th century used individual rights to fight for women's right to vote. Women argued that their right to equal protection under the law meant that they should have the same political rights as men. The passage of the 19th Amendment to the U.S. Constitution in 1920, which granted women the right to vote, was a victory for individual rights and a significant step towards gender equality.

The LGBTQ+ Rights Movement has used individual rights to fight against discrimination and oppression based on sexual orientation and gender identity. By invoking their right to equal protection under the law, LGBTQ+ individuals have challenged laws and practices that discriminate against them and demanded equal treatment under the law. The passage of laws and court decisions that recognize same-sex marriage and protect LGBTQ+ individuals from discrimination is a victory for individual rights.

Individual rights, particularly freedom of speech and assembly, are critical in promoting political participation and deliberation. These rights allow individuals to express their opinions and beliefs freely and openly without fear of persecution or discrimination. In a democratic society, this is crucial as it allows for the open exchange of ideas and perspectives, which is essential for informed decision-making and democratic governance.

Freedom of speech and assembly also enable individuals to engage in peaceful protests and demonstrations, which can be an effective way of bringing attention to issues and promoting political change. Without the protection of these individual rights, individuals may not feel free to express their opinions or engage in peaceful protest, which can stifle political participation and deliberation.

Individual rights are also essential for ensuring equal political participation in a democratic society. Without these rights, certain groups may be excluded or marginalized from the political process, which can undermine the legitimacy of democratic governance. Individual rights ensure that all individuals have the right to participate in the political process and have their voices heard, regardless of their race, gender, religion, or socioeconomic status.

Equal political participation is particularly important for promoting deliberation and informed decision-making. When all individuals have the opportunity to participate in the political process, a diverse range of perspectives and viewpoints are represented, which can lead to more informed decision-making and better policy outcomes. Without individual rights, certain groups may be excluded or marginalized from the political process, which can lead to policies that do not reflect the needs or interests of all citizens.

Individual rights also play a crucial role in promoting diverse viewpoints in the political process. By protecting freedom of speech and assembly, individuals are free to express their opinions and beliefs, even if they are unpopular or controversial. This can lead to a diversity of viewpoints in the political process, which is essential for promoting deliberation and informed decision-making.

Diverse viewpoints are particularly important in a democratic society, as they ensure that all perspectives are represented in the political process. Without these viewpoints, policies may only reflect the interests and needs of certain groups, which can lead to policies that are not in the best interests of all citizens. By protecting individual rights, a diversity of viewpoints can be represented in the political process, which can lead to policies that are more reflective of the needs and interests of all citizens.

Individual rights play a critical role in promoting political participation and deliberation in a democratic society. By protecting freedom of speech and assembly, ensuring equal political participation, and promoting diverse viewpoints, individual rights ensure that all individuals have the right to participate in the political process and have their voices heard. This is crucial for informed decision-making and democratic governance, as it ensures that policies reflect the needs and interests of all citizens, not just a select few.

Chapter 8: Economic Rights and Free Markets

The relationship between individual rights and free markets has been a topic of debate among philosophers, economists, and policymakers for centuries. The concept of individual rights refers to the rights and freedoms that every individual possesses by virtue of being a human being, while free markets refer to an economic system where individuals and businesses are free to buy, sell, and produce goods and services without government intervention.

Individual rights and free markets are often viewed as complementary concepts. Advocates of free markets argue that individual rights are best protected in a market-based economy because they promote individual autonomy, freedom of choice, and the ability to pursue one's own interests without government interference. In a free market, individuals are free to choose how they allocate their resources, what goods and services they consume, and what businesses they support. This freedom is seen as a fundamental aspect of individual rights.

Similarly, proponents of individual rights argue that free markets are necessary for the protection of individual rights. They argue that the ability to own property, make contracts, and engage in voluntary exchange is essential to the protection of individual rights. In a market-based economy, individuals have the ability to engage in economic transactions without government intervention, which promotes individual autonomy and the ability to exercise one's own rights.

However, critics of free markets argue that they can be detrimental to individual rights. They argue that in a market-based economy, the distribution of wealth and resources is often uneven, which can lead to the violation of individual rights. In a free market, individuals with more resources and power can dominate and exploit those with fewer resources, which can result in the violation of individual rights. Additionally, they argue that free markets can lead to the concentration of economic power, which can limit competition and undermine individual freedom and choice.

Despite these criticisms, many philosophers and economists argue that individual rights and free markets are compatible concepts. They argue that a free market economy can be designed in such a way that it promotes individual rights, while still ensuring that the distribution of resources and wealth is fair and just.

One argument for the compatibility of individual rights and free markets is based on the idea of property rights. Advocates of property rights argue that the ability to own and control property is a fundamental aspect of individual rights. In a free market economy, property rights are protected, which promotes individual autonomy and the ability to exercise one's own rights. Additionally, they argue that property rights promote economic growth and innovation, which benefits all members of society.

Another argument for the compatibility of individual rights and free markets is based on the idea of competition. Proponents of free markets argue that competition is essential to the protection of individual rights. They argue that competition ensures that businesses are held accountable for their actions, which promotes consumer protection and prevents the exploitation of individuals. Additionally, they argue that competition promotes innovation and efficiency, which benefits consumers and promotes economic growth.

Opponents of the notion that individual rights and free markets are compatible concepts put forth several arguments. Firstly, they contend that free markets can lead to economic inequality, which is often perpetuated due to the uneven distribution of resources and wealth. This, in turn, can lead to the infringement of individual rights. The inability of some individuals to access basic necessities, such as education and healthcare, due to economic disparities can result in the violation of their individual rights.

Secondly, critics argue that free markets can enable the concentration of economic power, which can limit competition and impede individual freedom and choice. When few entities or individuals dominate an industry or sector, they can exploit their position of power and infringe upon the rights of others. This can lead to the violation of individual rights, such as the right to engage in voluntary exchange or the right to fair competition.

Overall, these arguments suggest that the relationship between individual rights and free markets is not necessarily a harmonious one, and that measures must be taken to ensure that free markets are structured in a way that promotes and safeguards individual rights.

Property rights play a crucial role in economic freedom. Economic freedom is defined as the ability of individuals and businesses to engage in voluntary transactions and the freedom to produce, consume and trade goods and services without interference from the government. Property rights are the legal rights to use, own, and transfer property and assets.

One of the primary roles of property rights is to promote investment and economic growth. Property rights provide individuals and businesses with the legal framework to own and control assets and resources, which incentivizes investment and entrepreneurial activity. When individuals and businesses know that they have the legal right to own and control their property, they are more likely to invest in it and utilize it in a way that maximizes its value. This, in turn, promotes economic growth and development.

Moreover, property rights promote the efficient allocation of resources. When individuals and businesses have the legal right to own and control their property, they are more likely to use it efficiently and productively. This efficiency leads to an efficient allocation of resources within the economy. For instance, if a farmer has the legal right to own their land, they are more likely to invest in improving the productivity of the land by using advanced farming techniques and better equipment. This efficiency can then spill over to the entire economy, leading to better economic performance.

Additionally, property rights protect individuals and businesses from theft, fraud, and other illegal activities. Property rights provide a legal framework that makes it easier for individuals and businesses to seek legal recourse when their property is stolen or damaged. This protection encourages investment and productive activities since individuals and businesses can be confident that their property is secure.

However, it is important to note that property rights alone cannot guarantee economic freedom. The government must also provide a regulatory framework that supports the protection of property rights. The government should enforce laws that protect property rights and ensure that there is a functioning judicial system to adjudicate property disputes. This legal framework provides individuals and businesses with the confidence that their property rights will be protected and that they can engage in economic activity without fear of losing their property.

Property rights play a critical role in economic freedom. They promote investment, economic growth, and the efficient allocation of resources. They also protect individuals and businesses from illegal activities such as theft and fraud. However, it is crucial that the government enforces laws that protect property rights and provides a regulatory framework that supports their protection. By doing so, property rights can be used as a tool to promote economic freedom and growth.

Economic freedom refers to the ability of individuals and businesses to engage in voluntary transactions, produce, consume, and trade goods and services without interference from the government. The concept of economic freedom has been widely discussed in economic and political circles as a key factor in promoting economic growth and development.
One of the primary benefits of economic freedom is the promotion of entrepreneurship and innovation. Economic freedom provides individuals with the ability to pursue their interests and create new businesses, products, and services. In a free market, individuals are motivated to

innovate and take risks because they can keep the profits from their successes. This, in turn, leads to the creation of new jobs and products, which can stimulate economic growth.

Moreover, economic freedom promotes competition, which is a key driver of economic growth and innovation. In a free market, businesses must compete with one another to provide the best products or services at the lowest prices. This competition encourages businesses to innovate, lower prices, and improve the quality of their products, ultimately benefiting consumers.

Additionally, economic freedom promotes the efficient allocation of resources. When individuals and businesses have the freedom to produce and trade goods and services, resources are allocated more efficiently. In a free market, prices serve as signals of scarcity and demand. As such, resources are allocated to the most profitable uses, leading to a more efficient allocation of resources.

Furthermore, economic freedom is closely linked to personal freedom. In a free market, individuals have the freedom to choose how they will use their resources and what they will produce or consume. This freedom leads to a sense of autonomy and self-determination, which are important components of personal freedom.

Another benefit of economic freedom is the reduction of poverty. When individuals have the freedom to pursue their interests and participate in economic activity, they are more likely to generate income and create jobs. This, in turn, reduces poverty levels and increases the standard of living for individuals and society as a whole.

Furthermore, economic freedom can lead to greater international trade and cooperation. When countries have free markets, they are more likely to engage in international trade, which can promote economic growth and development on a global scale. Additionally, economic freedom can lead to greater cooperation between countries, as they seek to expand their economic opportunities and engage in mutually beneficial trade relationships.

However, it is important to note that economic freedom does not guarantee equal outcomes for all individuals. Some individuals may be more successful than others in a free market, leading to income inequality. Additionally, a lack of regulation can lead to negative externalities, such as pollution or labor exploitation.

Economic freedom provides numerous benefits for individuals and society as a whole. It promotes entrepreneurship, innovation, competition, efficient resource allocation, personal freedom, and the reduction of poverty. Furthermore, economic freedom can lead to greater international trade and cooperation. While there are potential drawbacks to economic freedom, such as income inequality and negative externalities, the benefits it provides cannot be ignored. As such, policymakers should strive to promote economic freedom while also addressing potential negative consequences.

Innovation and entrepreneurship are critical drivers of economic growth and development. They promote the creation of new businesses, products, and services, leading to increased employment opportunities and improved living standards.

Economic rights refer to the ability of individuals and businesses to engage in voluntary transactions and trade goods and services without interference from the government. Economic rights are closely linked to free markets, which provide the conditions for innovation and entrepreneurship to thrive. Free markets allow for the efficient allocation of resources and promote competition, which encourages businesses to innovate and take risks.

One of the primary ways in which economic rights and free markets promote innovation and entrepreneurship is by providing incentives for individuals and businesses to invest in research and development. In a free market, individuals and businesses are motivated to innovate and create new products and services because they can keep the profits from their successes. This incentive system encourages businesses to invest in research and development, leading to the creation of new technologies and products.

Moreover, economic rights and free markets provide individuals with the freedom to pursue their interests and create new businesses. In a free market, individuals are free to start businesses and pursue their entrepreneurial goals. This freedom encourages individuals to take risks and pursue innovative ideas, leading to the creation of new businesses and the expansion of existing ones.

Additionally, economic rights and free markets promote competition, which is a key driver of innovation and entrepreneurship. In a free market, businesses must compete with one another to provide the best products or services at the lowest prices. This competition encourages businesses to innovate, lower prices, and improve the quality of their products, ultimately benefiting consumers.

Furthermore, economic rights and free markets provide the conditions for small businesses to thrive. Small businesses are often the drivers of innovation and entrepreneurship, as they are more nimble and able to take risks than larger corporations. In a free market, small businesses have the opportunity to compete on a level playing field with larger corporations, leading to increased innovation and entrepreneurship.

Moreover, economic rights and free markets can lead to the creation of new industries and markets. In a free market, businesses are free to pursue new opportunities and create new industries, leading to the creation of new jobs and increased economic growth. For example, the emergence of the internet and e-commerce has led to the creation of new industries and markets, providing opportunities for innovative businesses to thrive.

However, it is important to note that economic rights and free markets do not guarantee equal outcomes for all individuals. Some individuals may be more successful than others in a free market, leading to income inequality. Additionally, a lack of regulation can lead to negative externalities, such as pollution or labor exploitation.

Economic rights and free markets provide the conditions for innovation and entrepreneurship to thrive. They promote the creation of new businesses, products, and services, leading to increased employment opportunities and improved living standards. Economic rights and free markets provide incentives for individuals and businesses to invest in research and development, promote competition, provide the conditions for small businesses to thrive, and can lead to the creation of new industries and markets. While there are potential drawbacks to economic rights and free markets, such as income inequality and negative externalities, the benefits they provide cannot be ignored. As such, policymakers should strive to promote economic rights and free markets while also addressing potential negative consequences.

Civil rights are a critical component of promoting social justice, as they ensure that individuals are not discriminated against based on their race, gender, sexual orientation, or other protected characteristics.

Civil rights refer to the legal and constitutional rights that are guaranteed to all individuals in a society. These rights are designed to protect individuals from discrimination and ensure that they are treated equally under the law. Civil rights include protections against discrimination in housing, employment, and education, as well as the right to vote, access to public accommodations, and the right to freedom of speech and assembly.

One of the primary reasons civil rights are essential in promoting social justice is that they provide a framework for creating more equitable societies. Civil rights ensure that individuals are not discriminated against based on their race, gender, or other protected characteristics, which can help to level the playing field and reduce systemic inequalities. By promoting equal treatment under the law, civil rights can help to break down barriers that prevent individuals from reaching their full potential.

Moreover, civil rights can also promote social justice by empowering marginalized communities. When individuals are protected by civil rights laws, they are better able to advocate for themselves and their communities. Civil rights laws provide a mechanism for holding individuals and organizations accountable for discriminatory behavior, which can help to deter discriminatory practices and promote social justice.

Additionally, civil rights can promote social justice by creating a more inclusive and diverse society. By protecting individuals from discrimination, civil rights laws can help to create a more inclusive and welcoming environment for all individuals.

This can lead to increased diversity in schools, workplaces, and other areas of society, which can promote social justice by reducing prejudice and promoting understanding.

Furthermore, civil rights can also promote social justice by promoting access to education and other opportunities. When individuals are protected by civil rights laws, they are better able to access education and other opportunities that can help them to achieve their full potential. This can help to break down barriers to social mobility and promote more equitable societies.

However, it is important to note that civil rights alone are not enough to promote social justice. In addition to civil rights protections, society must also address broader systemic inequalities, such as income inequality, lack of access to healthcare and education, and other forms of structural discrimination. Moreover, civil rights protections are only effective if they are enforced and implemented effectively. In some cases, civil rights laws may be poorly enforced or may not be enforced at all, leading to continued discrimination and inequality.

Civil rights are critical in promoting social justice. They provide a framework for creating more equitable societies by promoting equal treatment under the law, empowering marginalized communities, creating a more inclusive and diverse society, and promoting access to education and other opportunities. However, civil rights protections alone are not enough to promote social justice.

Society must also address broader systemic inequalities and ensure that civil rights protections are enforced and implemented effectively. By promoting civil rights and addressing broader inequalities, we can work towards creating more just and equitable societies.

The United States has a long and complex history of struggle for civil rights. From the earliest days of the country, there have been struggles over issues such as slavery, voting rights, and equal treatment under the law.

The struggle for African American rights has been a central theme in American history. From the earliest days of the country, African Americans were enslaved and denied basic human rights. The abolitionist movement emerged in the early 19th century and called for an end to slavery. The Civil War was fought in part over the issue of slavery, and the Emancipation Proclamation, signed by President Abraham Lincoln in 1863, declared that all slaves in the Confederate states were free.

However, the struggle for African American rights did not end with the abolition of slavery. After the Civil War, African Americans faced discrimination and segregation in many areas of life, including housing, employment, and education. Jim Crow laws were enacted in many Southern states to enforce racial segregation, and the Ku Klux Klan and other hate groups targeted African Americans with violence and intimidation.

The Civil Rights Movement, which emerged in the mid-20th century, sought to end racial discrimination and segregation. Led by figures such as Martin Luther King Jr., Rosa Parks, and Malcolm X, the Civil Rights Movement used nonviolent protest and civil disobedience to call attention to the injustices faced by African Americans.

The movement achieved many important victories, including the passage of the Civil Rights Act of 1964 and the Voting Rights Act of 1965, which prohibited discrimination based on race in housing, employment, education, and voting.

The women's suffrage movement was another important struggle for civil rights in the United States. Women had long been denied the right to vote and were often relegated to secondary roles in society. The women's suffrage movement emerged in the late 19th century and called for women's right to vote and participate in politics. Led by figures such as Susan B. Anthony and Elizabeth Cady Stanton, the movement used tactics such as lobbying, rallies, and civil disobedience to advance their cause.

The women's suffrage movement achieved a major victory in 1920 with the passage of the 19th Amendment, which granted women the right to vote. However, the struggle for women's rights did not end there. Women continued to face discrimination and inequality in many areas of life, including employment and education. The feminist movement emerged in the 1960s and sought to address these issues, advocating for equal pay, reproductive rights, and other issues related to gender equality.

The struggle for LGBTQ+ rights has been another important civil rights movement in the United States. LGBTQ+ individuals have long faced discrimination and marginalization, and were often subject to arrest and harassment by law enforcement. The modern LGBTQ+ rights movement emerged in the late 1960s and early 1970s, following the Stonewall riots in New York City.

The LGBTQ+ rights movement used tactics such as marches, rallies, and civil disobedience to call attention to issues such as discrimination, hate crimes, and the right to marry. The movement achieved many important victories, including the repeal of sodomy laws and the legalization of same-sex marriage.

Despite these victories, the struggle for LGBTQ+ rights is far from over. LGBTQ+ individuals still face discrimination and marginalization in many areas of life, including housing, employment, and healthcare. The fight for LGBTQ+ rights continues to be an important part of the struggle for civil rights in the United States.

The issue of civil rights has been a constant struggle throughout human history. Civil rights, in their simplest definition, are the rights that are afforded to every individual by virtue of their citizenship. These rights are designed to protect individuals from discrimination and to promote their equal treatment under the law. The importance of civil rights in promoting equality and inclusion cannot be overstated.

Despite numerous advancements in human rights, civil rights remain as important today as they have ever been. In the modern world, civil rights are critical in ensuring that every individual is treated equally, regardless of their race, gender, religion, or sexual orientation. Civil rights help to create a level playing field, and they ensure that every individual has equal access to education, employment, and other opportunities.

The fight for LGBTQ+ rights continues to be an ongoing struggle in many parts of the world. In countries where homosexuality is still criminalized, civil rights are critical in protecting the rights of LGBTQ+ individuals. Civil rights ensure that LGBTQ+ individuals are not discriminated against or subjected to violence simply because of their sexual orientation.

The fight for civil rights has a long and complex history that dates back centuries. One of the earliest recorded examples of civil rights can be traced back to the Magna Carta, a document signed in 1215 that established the rights of English barons and limited the power of the monarchy. The

Magna Carta helped to establish the idea of the rule of law, which is a fundamental principle of civil rights.

In the United States, the struggle for civil rights has been a long and difficult one. The country was founded on the principles of freedom and equality, yet these principles were not always extended to all citizens. For much of its history, the United States was characterized by discrimination and segregation, particularly against Black people.

The Civil Rights Movement of the 1950s and 1960s was a pivotal moment in the fight for civil rights in the United States. Led by figures such as Martin Luther King Jr., the movement sought to end racial segregation and discrimination, and to secure greater rights and protections for Black people. The movement was successful in achieving many of its goals, including the passage of the Civil Rights Act of 1964, which prohibited discrimination based on race, color, religion, sex, or national origin.

The impact of civil rights on society has been significant. Civil rights have helped to create a more just and equal society, one in which every individual has the opportunity to succeed regardless of their background. Civil rights have also helped to promote greater social cohesion and understanding, by breaking down barriers between different communities and promoting greater acceptance of diversity.

The impact of civil rights is evident in the many achievements of minority groups in the United States and around the world. For example, the election of Barack Obama as the first Black President of the United States was a major milestone in the fight for civil rights. Similarly, the achievements of women and LGBTQ+ individuals in politics, business, and other fields are a testament to the power of civil rights in promoting equality and inclusion.

Chapter 10: Individual Rights and International Relations

Individual rights are fundamental to the principles of international law and diplomacy. The protection of individual rights is considered essential to achieving a just and peaceful world, where individuals can live with dignity and freedom. The role of individual rights in international law and diplomacy is multifaceted, ranging from the promotion of human rights to the enforcement of international laws and treaties.

Human rights are considered an essential aspect of international law and diplomacy. They are considered universal and inalienable, meaning that they apply to all individuals regardless of their nationality, race, gender, or religion. Human rights include civil and political rights such as freedom of speech, religion, and assembly, as well as economic, social, and cultural rights such as the right to education, healthcare, and work. The promotion and protection of human rights are considered critical to achieving peace and stability, as well as the protection of vulnerable populations such as refugees and children.

The Role of International Law

International law is the body of rules and principles that govern the relationships between states and other international actors. The role of international law in protecting individual rights is significant. International law provides a framework for states to protect and promote human rights, as well as to hold states accountable for human rights violations. International law includes treaties, conventions, and customary law that establish legal obligations for states to respect, protect, and fulfill human rights. The International Covenant on Civil and Political Rights (ICCPR) and the International Covenant on Economic, Social and Cultural Rights (ICESCR) are examples of international treaties that protect human rights. The

Universal Declaration of Human Rights (UDHR) is a non-binding document that sets out the basic rights and freedoms that all individuals are entitled to, regardless of their nationality or race.

Diplomacy is the art of conducting negotiations between states, with the aim of achieving agreements or resolving disputes. Diplomacy plays a crucial role in protecting individual rights, as it provides a mechanism for states to address human rights violations and to promote human rights at the international level. Diplomacy can be used to negotiate treaties and conventions, as well as to facilitate the monitoring and enforcement of human rights. Diplomacy also provides a platform for states to express concerns about human rights violations and to call for action to address these violations.

Despite the importance of individual rights in international law and diplomacy, protecting these rights remains a significant challenge. One of the main challenges is the lack of compliance with international human rights laws and treaties. Some states fail to implement human rights laws and treaties, or they may only do so selectively. Another challenge is the lack of enforcement mechanisms for international human rights laws and treaties. Even when violations are identified, there may be no effective way to hold states accountable for these violations. Additionally, some states may use their sovereignty as a justification for violating human rights, arguing that they have the right to govern their own affairs without interference from other states.

Individual rights play a crucial role in international law and diplomacy. The promotion and protection of human rights are essential to achieving peace and stability, as well as to protecting vulnerable populations such as refugees and children. International law provides a framework for states to protect and promote human rights, while diplomacy provides a platform for states to address human rights violations and to promote human rights at the international level. However, protecting individual rights remains a significant challenge, with issues such as non-compliance and lack of enforcement mechanisms posing obstacles to achieving the goal of a world where all individuals can live with dignity and freedom.

Individual rights play a critical role in promoting global peace and security. The protection and promotion of individual rights are essential to fostering a just and peaceful world, where individuals can live with dignity and freedom. This essay will discuss the importance of individual rights in promoting global peace and security, focusing on how the protection of individual rights contributes to the prevention of conflicts, the resolution of conflicts, and the establishment of sustainable peace.

The protection of individual rights is essential to preventing conflicts from arising in the first place. Individuals who enjoy their rights, such as freedom of speech, assembly, and expression, are more likely to participate in political processes, making them feel more included in their societies. This inclusion can help to reduce tensions and grievances that can lead to conflicts. The protection of individual rights is also important for preventing discrimination and inequality, which can lead to social and economic disparities that may contribute to conflicts.

In addition, the promotion of individual rights can contribute to the prevention of violent extremism and terrorism. Violent extremist groups often target marginalized communities and exploit their grievances to recruit new members. By promoting individual rights, governments and civil society can address the root causes of violent extremism and prevent the spread of extremist ideologies.

Individual rights are also crucial in resolving conflicts. Conflicts often arise from violations of human rights, including the denial of basic rights such as freedom of expression, religion, and assembly. Addressing these violations and protecting individual rights can help to de-escalate tensions and create conditions for peaceful resolution. For example, the inclusion of marginalized groups in peace negotiations can help to address their grievances and ensure that their rights are protected in any peace agreement.

The protection of individual rights is also essential in transitional justice processes following the end of a conflict. Transitional justice mechanisms, such as truth commissions and reparations programs, can help to address human rights violations that occurred during the conflict and promote reconciliation. The recognition of individual rights is a critical component of these mechanisms and can help to restore the trust of communities in the state and promote long-term peace.

Individual rights are a critical component of establishing sustainable peace. Sustainable peace is characterized by the absence of violence and the presence of institutions that promote justice and inclusion. The protection of individual rights is essential to building these institutions and promoting a culture of respect for the rule of law.

Individual rights also contribute to the development of inclusive societies that respect diversity and promote social cohesion. Inclusive societies are essential for promoting peace, as they can help to reduce tensions and foster understanding between different groups. By ensuring that all individuals enjoy their rights, governments and civil society can promote social cohesion and build a foundation for sustainable peace.

Despite the importance of individual rights in promoting global peace and security, there are significant challenges to promoting and protecting these rights. One of the main challenges is the lack of compliance with international human rights laws and treaties. Some states fail to implement human rights laws and treaties, or they may only do so selectively. Another challenge is the lack of enforcement mechanisms for international human rights laws and treaties. Even when violations are identified, there may be no effective way to hold states accountable for these violations. Additionally, some states may use their sovereignty as a justification for violating human rights, arguing that they have the right to govern their own affairs without interference from other states.

Individual rights are essential to promoting global peace and security. The protection and promotion of individual rights can help to prevent conflicts, resolve conflicts, and establish sustainable peace. By addressing the root causes of conflict, promoting inclusion and justice, and building institutions that respect human rights, governments and civil society can create a world where all individuals can live with dignity and freedom.

Promoting individual rights in authoritarian regimes is a challenging task that requires a multi-faceted approach. Authoritarian regimes are characterized by a lack of political freedom, repression of civil society, and restrictions on freedom of expression and association. These regimes often prioritize maintaining their grip on power over the protection of individual rights.

One of the main challenges to promoting individual rights in authoritarian regimes is the restrictions on civil society. Authoritarian regimes often restrict the activities of civil society organizations, such as human rights groups, independent media, and non-governmental organizations. These organizations play a critical role in promoting individual rights and holding governments accountable for their actions. However, in authoritarian regimes, civil society organizations may be subject to harassment, intimidation, and legal action, making it difficult for them to operate effectively.

In addition, authoritarian regimes may restrict the funding and operations of civil society organizations by requiring them to register with the government or obtain approval for their activities. These requirements can be used as a pretext to target and harass organizations that are critical of the government or advocate for human rights.

Another challenge to promoting individual rights in authoritarian regimes is the suppression of dissent. Authoritarian regimes often restrict freedom of expression, association, and assembly, making it difficult for individuals to express their opinions or organize peaceful protests. Dissent can be met with repression, including arbitrary detention, torture, and extrajudicial killings. In some cases, the government may use violence to suppress dissent, as in the case of the 2011 Syrian uprising.

The suppression of dissent can also extend to the media, with authoritarian regimes using censorship and propaganda to control the narrative and limit access to information. This can make it difficult for individuals to access accurate information about their rights, government actions, and political developments.

A third challenge to promoting individual rights in authoritarian regimes is the lack of international support. Authoritarian regimes often have strategic importance, whether it is due to their natural resources, geopolitical position, or regional influence. As a result, international actors may be hesitant to challenge these regimes or to pressure them to respect individual rights.

In some cases, international actors may even support authoritarian regimes for their own strategic interests, as was the case during the Cold War, where the US and the Soviet Union supported authoritarian regimes in order to advance their geo-political agendas.

Addressing the challenges of promoting individual rights in authoritarian regimes requires a multi-faceted approach that involves civil society organizations, governments, and international actors. Civil society organizations play a critical role in advocating for individual rights and promoting awareness of the challenges faced by individuals living under authoritarian regimes. These organizations can also provide support to victims of human rights abuses and monitor government actions.

Governments also have a role to play in promoting individual rights. They can support civil society organizations and advocate for the protection of individual rights in international forums. Governments can also provide funding and technical assistance to civil society organizations working on human rights issues.

International actors can also contribute to promoting individual rights in authoritarian regimes. They can pressure authoritarian regimes to respect individual rights and impose targeted sanctions on individuals responsible for human rights abuses. International actors can also provide funding and technical assistance to civil society organizations and support the work of human rights defenders.

Promoting individual rights in authoritarian regimes is a challenging task that requires a multi-faceted approach. Addressing the challenges of promoting individual rights requires the involvement of civil society organizations, governments, and international actors. By working together, these actors can promote the protection of individual rights, hold governments accountable for their actions, and contribute to the establishment of a more open and democratic society as a whole.

Chapter 11: The Challenges to Individual Rights in the Modern World

Authoritarian regimes pose a significant threat to individual rights. These regimes often prioritize maintaining their grip on power over the protection of individual rights, leading to restrictions on freedom of expression, association, and assembly. Citizens may also be subject to arbitrary detention, torture, and extrajudicial killings. In addition, authoritarian regimes may target civil society organizations, independent media, and non-governmental organizations that advocate for human rights.

Authoritarian regimes may use various tactics to suppress dissent, including censorship, propaganda, and disinformation. These tactics can make it difficult for individuals to access accurate information about their rights and government actions.

Terrorism is another significant threat to individual rights. Terrorist groups often target civilians and non-combatants, leading to loss of life, injury, and psychological trauma. Terrorism can also have a chilling effect on individual rights, leading to increased surveillance, restrictions on freedom of movement, and increased security measures. In addition, terrorist attacks may be used as a pretext for governments to introduce emergency measures that restrict individual rights.

Terrorism can also lead to discrimination and stigmatization of certain groups, such as immigrants and minorities. This can lead to increased social tensions and polarization, further undermining individual rights.

Individual rights may also face threats from other sources, including poverty, inequality, and climate change. Poverty can limit access to education, healthcare, and employment, and restrict the ability of individuals to exercise their rights. Inequality can also limit access to opportunities and resources, leading to social exclusion and discrimination.

Climate change can also have a significant impact on individual rights, particularly for vulnerable populations. Extreme weather events, sea-level rise, and food shortages can lead to displacement, loss of livelihoods, and increased social unrest. These impacts can lead to restrictions on freedom of movement and increased surveillance.

The threats to individual rights from authoritarianism, terrorism, and other sources can have a significant impact on society. These threats can lead to a breakdown of trust between individuals and the state, leading to increased social tensions and instability. Restrictions on individual rights can also undermine democracy and the rule of law, leading to a culture of impunity and disregard for human rights.

The impact of these threats can be particularly severe for vulnerable populations, such as women, children, and minorities. These groups may face discrimination, violence, and social exclusion, limiting their ability to exercise their rights and participate in society.

Individual rights are essential for the protection of human dignity and the promotion of freedom, justice, and equality. However, these rights face numerous threats from various sources, including authoritarianism, terrorism, and other factors. The impact of these threats can be severe, leading to a breakdown of trust between individuals and the state and undermining democracy and the rule of law. Addressing these threats requires a multi-faceted approach that involves civil society organizations, governments, and international actors. By working together, these actors can promote the protection of individual rights and contribute to the establishment of more open and democratic societies.

Technology has revolutionized our world in many ways, but it has also challenged individual rights in various ways. From privacy concerns to the impact of social media on freedom of expression, the role of technology in challenging individual rights is significant.

Privacy is one of the most significant individual rights that technology has challenged. The increasing use of technology in our daily lives, from smartphones to social media, has led to the collection and storage of vast amounts of personal data. This data can be used for various purposes, including targeted advertising, surveillance, and monitoring. The use of biometric data, such as facial recognition, has raised additional concerns about the potential for abuse.

The lack of effective regulation of data privacy has led to the exploitation of personal data by companies and governments. The Cambridge Analytica scandal, where the data of millions of Facebook users was collected without their knowledge or consent, is just one example of how technology can be used to undermine individual privacy rights.

The impact of technology on freedom of expression is complex. On the one hand, technology has allowed individuals to express themselves in ways that were previously impossible, from social media to blogging. However, the use of algorithms to promote certain content over others and the spread of fake news has raised concerns about the impact of technology on the quality of public discourse.

In addition, governments and other actors have used technology to suppress freedom of expression, from internet censorship to the use of spyware to monitor activists and journalists. The use of deepfake technology, which allows for the manipulation of videos and images, has also raised concerns about the potential for technology to be used to spread disinformation and propaganda.

Technology has also challenged the right to access information. While the internet has provided access to a wealth of information, the use of filters and algorithms can limit the type of information that individuals can access. The use of paywalls and subscription services has also limited access to certain types of information, particularly in the context of journalism.

In addition, the use of technology to manipulate search results and the spread of fake news has raised concerns about the impact of technology on the quality and accuracy of information. This can limit the ability of individuals to make informed decisions and participate in democratic processes.

The impact of technology on individual rights has a significant impact on society. The lack of privacy protections can lead to a culture of surveillance and undermine trust between individuals and the state. The impact of technology on freedom of expression can lead to the spread of disinformation and the erosion of democratic values. The limitations on access to information can limit the ability of individuals to make informed decisions and participate in democratic processes.

Technology has revolutionized our world in many ways, but it has also challenged individual rights in various ways. From privacy concerns to the impact of social media on freedom of expression, the role of technology in challenging individual rights is significant. The impact of these challenges can be severe, leading to the erosion of democratic values and a culture of surveillance. Addressing these challenges requires a multi-faceted approach that involves regulation, technological solutions, and individual actions.

The protection of individual rights is a cornerstone of democracy. Democracy requires that individuals have the right to participate in the political process, express their opinions freely, and have access to accurate and reliable information. Protecting individual rights ensures that individuals can exercise their right to participate in democratic processes without fear of retribution or repression.

Moreover, the protection of individual rights promotes democratic values such as equality and fairness. When individual rights are protected, all individuals are treated equally under the law, and the rule of law is upheld. This ensures that society is fair and just, and individuals have equal opportunities to succeed.

The protection of individual rights is critical in ensuring social justice. Social justice requires that all individuals have access to basic human needs such as education, healthcare, and housing. When individual rights are protected, individuals have access to the resources necessary to ensure that their basic needs are met. Moreover, the protection of individual rights ensures that all individuals are treated with dignity and respect, regardless of their social status or background.

The protection of individual rights is essential in promoting economic growth. When individual rights are protected, individuals can participate freely in economic activities without fear of repression or exploitation. This ensures that individuals can engage in entrepreneurial activities, which promote innovation and economic growth.

Moreover, the protection of individual rights ensures that markets are open and competitive. This ensures that businesses operate in an environment where there is a level playing field, which promotes innovation and economic growth.

The protection of individual rights is crucial in protecting human dignity. Human dignity requires that all individuals are treated with respect and have the right to make decisions about their lives. Protecting individual rights ensures that individuals have the autonomy to make decisions about their lives without fear of coercion or repression.

Moreover, the protection of individual rights ensures that individuals are treated with dignity and respect, regardless of their social status or background. This ensures that society is fair and just, and individuals are treated as valuable members of society.

The protection of individual rights is critical in promoting democracy, social justice, economic growth, and human dignity. Protecting individual rights ensures that individuals can participate freely in political and economic activities, access basic human needs, and are treated with dignity and respect. The challenges of authoritarianism, terrorism, and technological advances make protecting individual rights increasingly critical. It is important that individuals, civil society, and governments work together to promote the protection of individual rights and ensure that society is just and equitable.

Individual freedom is one of the most cherished values in modern society. However, freedom is not absolute and can be limited by laws, customs, and social norms. In order to protect individual freedom, it is necessary for individuals to take responsibility for their actions and to respect the rights and freedoms of others.

1. **Understanding Freedom:** In order to understand the importance of individual

responsibilities in protecting freedom, it is necessary to have a clear understanding of what freedom means. Freedom is the ability to act or think as one wishes without being constrained by external factors. However, freedom also implies responsibility. When individuals exercise their freedom, they must also be responsible for the consequences of their actions.

2. **The Importance of Laws:** Laws are necessary to protect individual freedom. Laws establish a framework of rules and regulations that limit the power of the state and protect the rights of individuals. However, laws alone are not enough to protect freedom. Individuals must also take responsibility for their actions and respect the rights of others. When individuals act in a responsible manner, they contribute to a society that is free and just.

3. **The Importance of Social Norms:** Social norms are unwritten rules of behavior that are enforced by social pressure. Social norms can be used to protect individual freedom by promoting responsible behavior and discouraging actions that harm others. For example, social norms against discrimination and bigotry can help to protect the freedom of individuals who belong to marginalized groups. By promoting responsible behavior, social norms can help to create a society that is free and fair.

4. **The Role of Education:** Education plays a critical role in promoting responsible behavior and protecting individual freedom. Education helps individuals to understand the value of freedom and the importance of respecting the rights of others. Education also provides individuals with the skills and knowledge necessary to make informed

decisions and to act in a responsible manner. By promoting education, societies can create a culture of responsibility that protects individual freedom.

5. **The Importance of Civic Engagement:** Civic engagement is the participation of individuals in the political and social affairs of their community. Civic engagement is important for protecting individual freedom because it allows individuals to influence the laws and policies that affect their lives. By participating in the democratic process, individuals can help to ensure that their rights and freedoms are protected. Civic engagement also promotes responsible behavior by encouraging individuals to take an active role in their community.

6. **The Importance of Personal Responsibility:** Personal responsibility is the willingness of individuals to take responsibility for their actions and to respect

the rights and freedoms of others. Personal responsibility is essential for protecting individual freedom because it promotes responsible behavior and discourages actions that harm others. When individuals act in a responsible manner, they contribute to a society that is free and just. Personal responsibility also helps to create a culture of responsibility that promotes individual freedom.

Individual freedom is a fundamental value in modern society. However, freedom is not absolute and can be limited by laws, customs, and social norms. In order to protect individual freedom, it is necessary for individuals to take responsibility for their actions and to respect the rights and freedoms of others. By promoting responsible behavior, education, civic engagement, and personal responsibility, societies can create a culture of responsibility that protects individual freedom.

The United States of America is a federal republic, comprising 50 states, a federal district, and several territories. It is considered one of the most powerful countries in the world, not just militarily and economically but also politically. One of the significant reasons behind its global supremacy is its system of government. The US has a presidential system of government, where the executive, legislative, and judicial branches function independently.

The US system of government is rooted in the principles of democracy and freedom, and it is designed to ensure that no one branch or individual has absolute power. The Constitution of the United States, which serves as the supreme law of the land, provides the framework for the federal government's powers and limitations. The Constitution divides the powers of the government into three branches: the legislative, executive, and judicial branches. This division of powers is known as the separation of powers, which ensures that no one branch has too much power and that the government's authority is distributed.

The legislative branch of the US government is responsible for making laws. It is composed of two houses of Congress: the Senate and the House of Representatives. The Senate is made up of two senators from each state, while the House of Representatives is based on the population of each state. The bicameral structure of Congress ensures that both large and small states have equal representation in the government. Furthermore, the Constitution provides that all revenue bills must originate in the House of Representatives, ensuring that the people's representatives have control over the government's purse strings.

The executive branch of the US government is responsible for enforcing the laws. The President of the United States is the head of the executive branch, and the Vice President, Cabinet members, and other officials support him. The President is responsible for foreign policy, domestic administration, and military affairs. The President's power is limited by the Constitution, which provides for a system of checks and balances. The President must work with Congress to enact laws, and his executive orders and decisions are subject to review by the judiciary.

The judicial branch of the US government is responsible for interpreting the laws. The Supreme Court of the United States is the highest court in the land, and it has the final say on legal matters. The Supreme Court is made up of nine justices appointed by the President and confirmed by the Senate. The Constitution grants the Supreme Court the power of judicial review, allowing it to declare laws or executive actions unconstitutional.

The system of government in the United States is designed to ensure that all citizens have the freedom to participate in the democratic process. The government operates under the rule of law, where no one is above the law, and everyone is equal under the law. This system of government provides for the protection of individual rights, including freedom of speech, religion, and the press. It also provides for the protection of property rights and the right to a fair trial.

The US system of government is unique because it balances individual rights with the common good. The government provides for the general welfare of the people, while also ensuring that individual rights are not violated. This system of government is critical to the preservation of freedom and democracy in the United States.

Another essential feature of the US system of government is federalism. The federal system of government provides for a balance of power between the federal government and the state governments. The Constitution grants certain powers to the federal government, while reserving other powers to the states. This division of powers ensures that the federal government cannot infringe on the rights of the states or the people.

The United States of America is known for its commitment to freedom, liberty, and democracy. From its founding, the country has been dedicated to these ideals and has fought for them at home and abroad. As a result, American freedom has become a beacon of hope for people all around the world, who look to the United States as a model of what is possible in terms of individual rights, political representation, and social justice.

The idea of freedom has been central to American identity since the country's founding. The Declaration of Independence, which was signed on July 4, 1776, states that "all men are created equal, that they are endowed by their Creator with certain unalienable Rights, that among these are Life,

Liberty and the pursuit of Happiness." This bold statement declared the principles upon which the United States was founded and set the stage for the country's ongoing struggle to realize those principles in practice.

Throughout American history, there have been many struggles to expand and defend freedom. The American Revolution, which was fought between 1775 and 1783, was a rebellion against British rule that was motivated by a desire for greater political freedom. The Civil War, which was fought between 1861 and 1865, was a conflict over the issue of slavery that ultimately led to the abolition of slavery and the enshrinement of the principle of equality under the law. The Civil Rights Movement of the 1950s and 1960s was another struggle for freedom, this time focused on securing equal rights and opportunities for African Americans.

The commitment to freedom and democracy that has been central to American identity has had a profound impact on global politics and culture. The United States has played a leading role in promoting democracy and human rights around the world, often through military intervention or economic aid. For example, the United States played a key role in the defeat of fascism in World War II and the subsequent reconstruction of Europe through the Marshall Plan. More recently, the United States has been involved in conflicts in Iraq and Afghanistan, with the stated goal of promoting democracy and stability in those countries.

In addition to its role in global politics, American freedom has had a significant impact on popular culture around the world. American movies, music, and television shows are popular in many countries, and the ideals of freedom and individualism that are often portrayed in these media have had a significant influence on how people around the world think about themselves and their societies.

Despite the important role that American freedom has played in global politics and culture, there are also many challenges and opportunities that lie ahead for this important ideal. One of the biggest challenges is the ongoing struggle to expand and protect civil liberties in the United States. In recent years, there have been concerns about the erosion of civil liberties in the name of national security, as well as debates over issues such as immigration and the rights of LGBTQ+ individuals.

Another challenge is the rise of authoritarianism and populism around the world, which threatens to undermine the principles of freedom and democracy that the United States has long championed. Countries such as Russia, China, and Turkey have become increasingly authoritarian in recent years, and the United States must navigate these challenges while remaining committed to its principles.

Democracy has several benefits that make it a preferred form of governance for many people. One of the most important benefits of democracy is that it provides individuals with a voice in government. Through elections, citizens are able to choose their representatives, and hold them accountable for their actions. This means that citizens have a direct say in how their government is run, and can work to ensure that their interests are represented.

Another benefit of democracy is that it encourages political stability. In a democratic system, power is distributed among different branches of government, and checks and balances are put in place to prevent any one person or group from gaining too much power. This helps to ensure that no single individual or group can monopolize political power, and prevents the kind of instability and violence that can result from authoritarian regimes.

Finally, democracy has been shown to promote economic growth and development. Studies have shown that countries with more democratic systems tend to have higher levels of economic growth, lower levels of corruption, and more stable institutions. This is because democratic systems tend to be more transparent and accountable, which helps to attract investment and promote economic development.

Democracy is a form of government that allows citizens to participate in the decision-making process of the country. In a democratic government, citizens have the right to elect their leaders, express their opinions, and hold their leaders accountable. Authoritarianism, on the other hand, is a form of government in which all power is held by one individual or a small group of individuals, who have little or no accountability to the citizens they govern.

One of the primary reasons why democracy should be preserved is that it provides a system of checks and balances that prevents abuses of power. In a democratic government, power is divided among different branches, each with its own set of responsibilities. For example, in the United States, power is divided among the executive, legislative, and judicial branches. This division of power ensures that no one branch becomes too powerful, and that each branch can act as a check on the others. This system of checks and balances is essential for preventing abuses of power and protecting the rights of citizens.

Authoritarianism, on the other hand, concentrates power in the hands of one individual or a small group of individuals. This concentration of power can lead to abuses of power, corruption, and oppression. Without a system of checks and balances, there is little to prevent those in power from abusing their authority. This can lead to the suppression of dissent, the persecution of minorities, and the violation of basic human rights.

Another reason why democracy should be preserved is that it promotes transparency and accountability. In a democratic government, leaders are accountable to the people they govern. They are elected by the people, and they must answer to the people for their actions. This accountability promotes transparency, as leaders must be open and honest about their actions and decisions. This transparency helps to build trust between the government and the people.

Authoritarianism, on the other hand, lacks accountability and transparency. Leaders in an authoritarian government are not elected by the people, and they do not answer to the people for their actions. This lack of accountability can lead to corruption and abuse of power, as leaders have no one to answer to. Without transparency, there is no way for the people to know what their leaders are doing, which can lead to suspicion and mistrust.

A third reason why democracy should be preserved is that it promotes stability and prosperity. In a democratic government, the rule of law is paramount. Laws are created through a democratic process, and they are enforced by an independent judiciary. This creates a stable and predictable environment that is conducive to economic growth and prosperity.

Authoritarianism, on the other hand, is often characterized by instability and unpredictability. Leaders in an authoritarian government are not bound by the rule of law, and they can change the rules at any time to suit their own interests. This unpredictability can lead to economic instability and uncertainty, which can harm businesses and discourage investment.

A fourth reason why democracy should be preserved is that it promotes human rights and dignity. In a democratic government, the rights of citizens are protected by law. Citizens have the right to express their opinions, worship as they choose, and live their lives as they see fit. These rights are protected by an independent judiciary, which can hold the government accountable if it violates these rights.

Authoritarianism, on the other hand, often leads to the suppression of human rights and dignity. Leaders in an authoritarian government often see themselves as above the law, and they are willing to use any means necessary to maintain their power. This can lead to the persecution of minorities, the suppression of dissent, and the violation of basic human rights.